101 THINGS TO DO IN A SHED

Hours of Fun for Boys of All Ages!

Published in 2006 by
Stewart, Tabori & Chang
115 West 18th Street
New York, NY 10011
www.abramsbooks.com

Library of Congress Cataloging-in-Publication Data is on file with the Library of Congress

ISBN: 1-58479-493-3

Illustrations by Steven Bannister
Designed by Lindsey Johns

Printed and bound in China

10 9 8 7 6 5 4 3 2 1

First Printing

Conceived, designed and produced by
Quid Publishing
Level Four
Sheridan House
114 Western Road
Hove BN3 1DD
England
www.quidpublishing.com

Note: Every effort has been made to ensure that all information contained in this book is correct and compatible with national standards at the time of publication. This book is not intended to replace manufacturers' instructions on the use of their tools and products. Always follow their safety guidelines.

The author, publisher, and copyright holder assume no responsibility for any injury, loss, or damage caused or sustained as a consequence of the use and application of the contents of this book.

Stewart, Tabori & Chang is a subsidiary of

101 THINGS TO DO IN A SHED

Contents Include:

- ✈ **Making Models**
- ✕ **Hand Tool Techniques**
- ◉ **Science Experiments**
- ⚠ **Tricks and Games**
- ⛵ **Weekend Projects**
- ✿ **How Things Work**

ROB BEATTIE

Stewart, Tabori & Chang
New York

CONTENTS

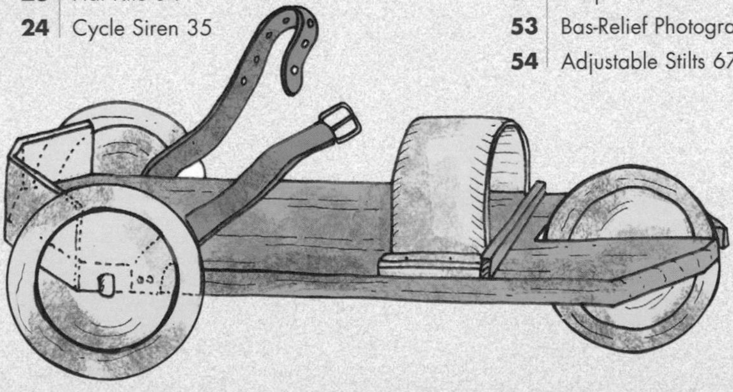

Project 100
Scooter Skate,
page 121

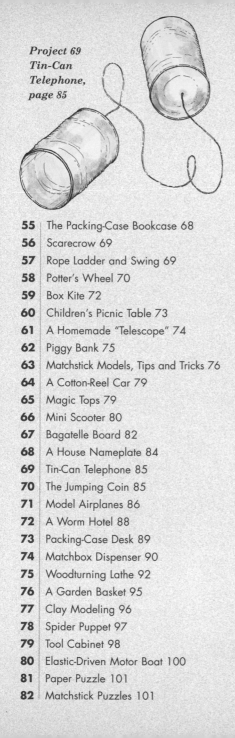

*Project 69
Tin-Can
Telephone,
page 85*

*Project 46
Chair Ladder,
page 58*

INTRODUCTION

"Every man should have a shed," a neighbor of ours once pronounced in a tone that made it clear that this was a place her partner could be banished to, rather than somewhere he would actively seek out. What she didn't realize, of course, was that she was playing into his hands.

Every man should indeed have a shed, whether you use it for putting your feet up and listening to a battered old transistor radio on a Sunday afternoon, or for masterminding your assault on the local horticultural fair, building the only railroad in the neighborhood that actually runs on time, or—and here's where this book comes in—making stuff. You see, despite the current vogue for recasting the shed as a kind of prefabricated, flat-pack cave where postmodern man can "find himself," he's actually more interested in finding things to do. That's what our fathers and grandfathers knew. That's what a shed is for.

This book came about because of a desire to try to re-create the style and substance of those

Boy's Own Annuals that enthralled preteens and teenagers from the 1920s and '30s onwards. As such, it's a small part of the backlash against 21st-century culture, where kids are force-fed lowest-common-denominator pap designed to glue their backsides to the sofa, rather than putting their brains into gear.

We also wanted to produce something that had a nostalgic element to it and that, like those early *Boy's Own* books, didn't necessarily fill in all the gaps. That's why you'll find some of these projects require you to think for yourself

Take one shed, add this book, and you'll instantly have 101 things to do. And that's just the start...

*Making things
the traditional
way is much
more fun.*

a bit, rather than just following step-by-step instructions. Part of the beauty of shed work, you see, is improvisation—working out ways around particular problems for yourself and coming up with innovative or alternative solutions.

That's not to say you'll need too much guesswork, because nearly everything here is supplied with measurements in imperial and metric, along with suggestions for the best kind of wood or metal to use, and instructions and diagrams that show how things fit together.

We've also stuck mainly to describing how a particular job can be done using simple hand tools, rather than getting into the modern, powered alternatives. This is partly to show that you don't need to spend a lot of money to make something useful or fun, and partly because the more traditional approach brings its own rewards. Making a dovetailed joint the old fashioned way is much more satisfying than just turning on a router and dialling in the correct measurements.

So, in the pages that follow you'll find all sorts of woodwork projects that you can build, experiments that you can observe, along with tricks and puzzles you can play on your friends. We hope we've managed to find a decent balance between the classics—catapult, cotton-reel tank, scooter, model planes,

boats and so on—and some ideas you might not have thought of—worm hotel, spring-trap car, kaleidoscope, a woodturning lathe, home-made stationery and a potter's wheel.

If the ones you like look a bit complicated at first, start with a few of the easy ones and you'll soon get the hang of it; as we said before, part of the fun here should be learning from your mistakes. You'll also find that we refer to one or two things that were more commonplace in the past than they are today. Finding a good source of old-fashioned wooden packing cases may tax you almost as much as making something out of them; similarly, tracking down a hardware store that's still willing to make some of the one-off bits and pieces described here may require a bit of detective work, but that's part of the fun too.

Why? Because every man needs to solve problems and to make things. In short, every man needs a shed.

*The key to running
a tight shed: keep your
tools squared neatly away.*

① WORKING WITH WOOD

Broadly speaking, there are seven types of wood that will serve most purposes—hardwood, softwood, blockboard, chipboard, hardboard, medium-density fiberboard (MDF) and plywood.

Hardwood types include ash, beech, cherry, oak mahogany, teak and walnut. It's more expensive than softwood because it lasts longer, and is often used by furniture makers. Good hardwood is seasoned and then "stick-dried"—see Fig. 1—and it usually pays to buy the dirtiest, oldest-looking bits you can find. Typical softwoods include cedar, pine and spruce; though cheaper than hardwood, they're not so durable and need protecting if you're using them for an outside project. Imperfections are common in softwood and although you can get around knots—even if you have to scrap the bit of wood with the knot in it—it's harder to deal with wood that's warped or twisted.

Of the others, blockboard is actually strips of softwood glued and bonded under high pressure, then bookended by veneer to form a "sandwich." Cheap and adaptable, chipboard is made from bits of softwood coated in resin, fused together under pressure; hardboard is softwood pulp that's forced into sheets under pressure. MDF has gotten bad press recently but it's an extremely versatile "wood" for all indoor work and safe enough for our purposes, if you wear a mask. Plywood is made by bonding uneven numbers of veneers together and comes in various types and thicknesses—including weatherproof versions for use outside.

If you're concerned about the environment—good for you—you can start by trying to restore something that already exists or by buying reclaimed or "waste" timber. If you want new timber then start by looking for something that's certified as coming from a well-managed forest. This will vary depending on where you live—in the UK, for example, look for wood that's FSC (Forest Stewardship Council) certified.

One final point. Always store wood for a day or two in the place where you're going to be working on it—wood that's been stored outside may shrink when you bring it indoors.

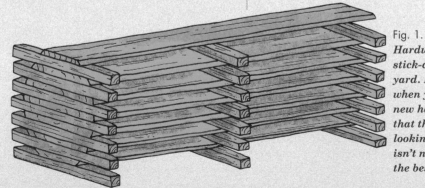

Fig. 1.
Hardwood being stick-dried in a yard. Remember when you buy new hardwood that the nice-looking stuff isn't necessarily the best.

② MEASURING

Being able to measure your materials accurately is one of the keys to successful wood and metalworking.

For this you'll need an ordinary straight ruler with clear, easy-to-read markings in both metric and imperial; metal rulers last longer, are harder to damage and easier to clean—shoe polish is a good way to highlight the markings. You will probably use a 12 or 24 in. (300 or 600 mm) ruler the most, but for longer measurements an extending metal tape measure is best; if you prefer something more solid, then folding rulers work well. You can even buy a digital tape measure—but, hey, where's the fun in that?

An ordinary ruler is no use if you need to make a square cut—for example, off the end of a piece of wood. For this you need a try square. Start by marking one of the broad sides with a single pencil stroke, then do both sides, and finally mark the other broad side. This will ensure you get a true square cut. Try squares are also good for checking that corners you've made yourself are true; for measuring 45-degree angles, get a miter square. If you're having trouble marking up

wood with a pencil, try a trimming knife instead—this scores the wood and provides a key for the first saw cut.

A compass and protractor are useful for making small circles; for larger ones, you can drill a series of holes in a ruler, then fit a nail in one to act as a pivot and a pencil in another at the appropriate distance away—you just rotate the ruler around the nail.

Use a spirit level for making sure that wood is level, and if your shelves are straight but the wall isn't, try this. Hold the shelf against the wall and place a small wooden block on top of it. Hold a pencil against the block and then push both block and pencil from one end of the shelf to the other—the resulting line will show you where to cut the shelf so it fits exactly. Finally, remember to "dry-fit" joints before gluing them to make sure that your measurements are accurate.

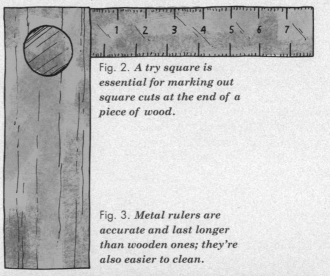

Fig. 2. *A try square is essential for marking out square cuts at the end of a piece of wood.*

Fig. 3. *Metal rulers are accurate and last longer than wooden ones; they're also easier to clean.*

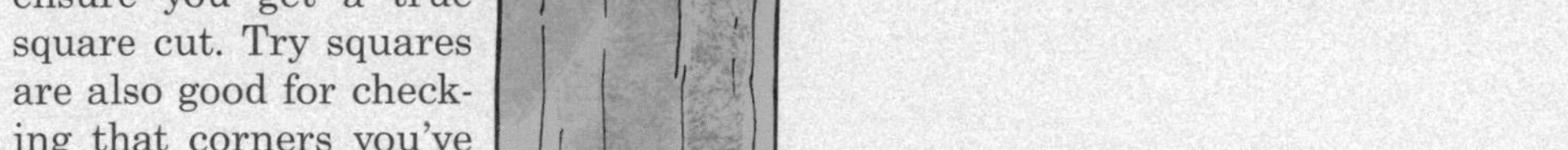

③ NAILING, SCREWING AND GLUING

Should you be bold enough to attempt every project here, you'll find yourself doing a lot of nailing, screwing and gluing, so it's a good idea to pause for a moment and absorb some good practice.

Broadly speaking, nails are used for rough constructions, screws for high-class fixing (or where a joint needs to be particularly robust) and glue for fixing narrow pieces of wood or to support a nailed joint.

Like most aspects of woodwork—which is, after all, a mixture of art, science and experience—there are no hard-and-fast rules. Of all the different kinds of nail, the oval brad is probably the most useful for general work, while the panel pin is used most often for small, fine joints; you'll also find a few tin tacks used in these pages.

Oval brads should be nailed with the narrow side running along the grain so as to avoid splitting the wood—fit them this way and you can even drive them into wood close to the ends without splitting. One caveat here: if you're nailing towards the end of a piece of wood and are concerned about splitting it, use a bradawl to start the hole off.

As a rule, you need to drive nails in vertically by holding the hammer at the end—holding it near the head makes you feel like you have more control but doesn't actually give you any—and hitting the nail squarely on the head; hold short nails in place with the teeth of a comb. If you're clever,

you can hide a nail by first lifting a sliver of wood like a hinge with a gouge, driving the nail home into the space underneath and then gluing the sliver back to hide the nail. If you bend a nail and need to get it out, put a scrap piece of wood between your claw hammer and the wood the nail is embedded in—that way, you'll mark the scrap wood and not the real thing.

There are only basically two kinds of screws—round and flat-head. Flat screws are designed to be countersunk so that they lay flat to the surface of the wood, while round heads are usually for attaching metal fittings and so don't need to be flush (anyway, brass screws look rather nice). With large screws, it's advis-

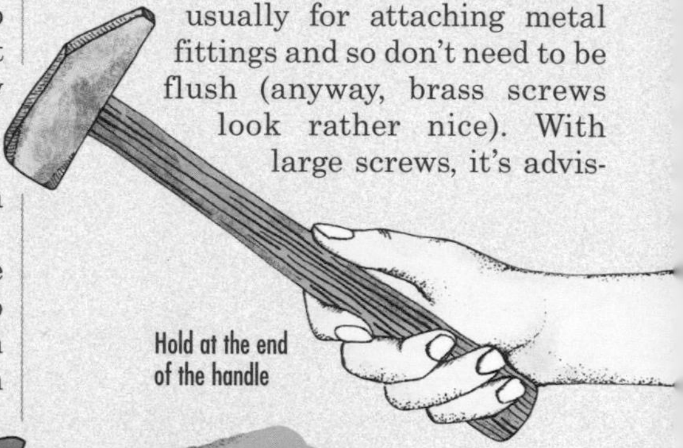

Hold at the end
of the handle

Fig. 4. *If you use oval brads, make sure you nail them with the narrow side running along the grain.*

10

able to start the hole off first of all with a bradawl or a drill, and if you're using brass screws in stiff wood, try sinking a steel screw of exactly the same size first—then you can remove it and replace it with the brass screw. Some people also recommend rolling screws in candle wax, Vaseline or grease first—don't use soap, as it can react with the wood. If you've botched getting a screw in and it's loose, poke a spent match into the hole and snap it off, then try again.

A final word on screwdrivers: unless space is tight, remember that longer screwdrivers offer more leverage, and always check that the tip of your screwdriver is in good condition and make sure it offers the best fit—otherwise you'll damage the screw.

Most of the projects in the this book can be done using standard wood glue, usually called either polyurethane or PVA glue—just watch out that you get the waterproof version if it's for use outside.

Although you can use glue straight from the pot, a fiber brush will actually ensure a smoother, more even coating. If you're gluing a joint, brush both pieces of wood at the same time and then rub them back and forth against each other—you can also wipe off any excess glue with a damp cloth at this stage. When you feel them start to take, there should still be enough movement left in the joint for you to position exactly and leave it to set. Don't use too much glue.

If the joint is made up of thin wood—or isn't very accurate—you shouldn't really just leave it. Instead, you can either use a store-bought clamp or make something up yourself as described in the picture-framing project on pages 24–25.

Gluing is also about preparation, and you should take care to plane any wood that you need to glue perfectly square so that you can't see any daylight when you hold them together. If you're putting joints together, "dry-fit" them first to make sure that they go together properly.

Fig. 5. *Apply glue with a brush to get a more even and longer-lasting coating.*

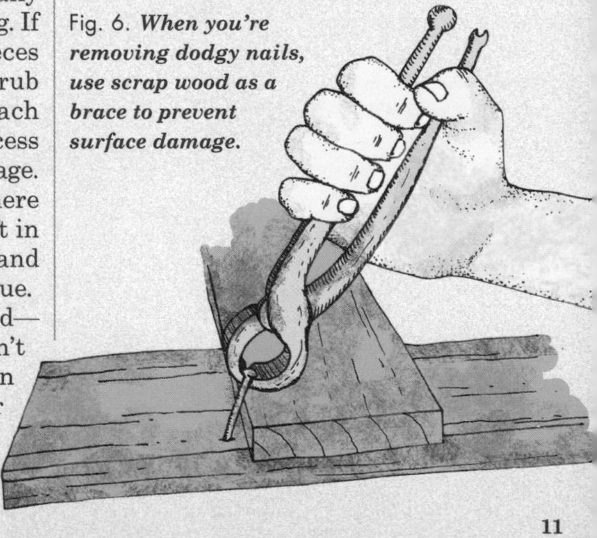

Fig. 6. *When you're removing dodgy nails, use scrap wood as a brace to prevent surface damage.*

4 SAWING MADE SIMPLE

Because sawing appears so simple—move sharp edge of saw vigorously against the thing you want to cut and eventually it will come apart—everyone thinks they'll be able to do it, straight out of the box. The fact that most people can't is usually down to using the wrong saw, using one that's blunt, not holding it properly, or applying the wrong kind of pressure.

You can probably get by with four saws (five if you want to do fretwork, see pages 16–17): a handsaw for cutting up planks, a tenon saw (nice stiff back and good for sawing smaller pieces of wood accuately), a keyhole saw for handling curves, and a hacksaw to get through metal.

Whatever kind you're using, make sure you hold it properly. Your first fin-

ger should point along the handle to keep it steady, while your left hand—usually, anyway—holds the piece of wood to stop it wobbling. If you're feeling confident, hold your left thumb against the side of the blade to help keep it straight when you make the first cut. You should hold a keyhole saw with both hands on its handle and a hacksaw with one hand holding the screw at the front of the frame.

You need to saw with long, smooth strokes, rather than short little stabs. Don't press down too hard—if you're getting the action right, there's no need to. Bad technique simply blunts the saw more quickly and produces a rough, crooked edge. Remember: women admire a man who saws with success.

Start your cut as gently as you can by moving the saw back and forth over the wood until it bites, and when you're about to finish the cut, ease up, make sure that the wood doesn't "hinge" open and don't put any pressure on the saw—the teeth should do the job for you.

Look after your saws by hanging them or stacking them in a special rack so they don't twist. If they're going to be out of action for a while, a little grease will keep the rust off.

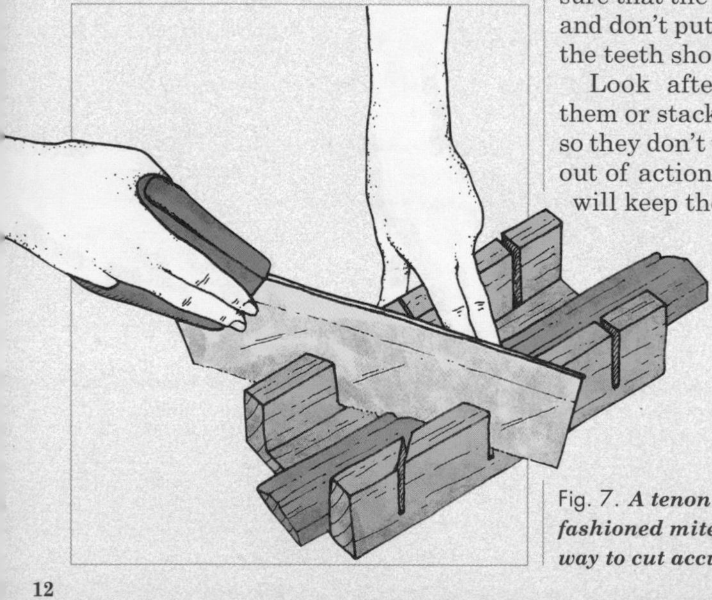

Fig. 7. *A tenon saw and old-fashioned miter block—a great way to cut accurate angles.*

⑤ CARVING, TURNING, AND BEVELING

As well as being practical, a project needs to look as good as you can get it. You may never be a total master of the craft, but you can do yourself and your woodwork a few favors by finishing off properly.

Beveling, where you make a flat surface by cutting off the edge or a corner of a section of wood is both decorative and practical. It introduces angles to items that would otherwise be composed entirely of straight lines and right angles, and as a by-product can help stop some woods from splitting. Obviously, you bevel the edges of things—typically at the top and bottom of something like a bookcase or a table—and in the days before power tools, you'd have used something called a bevel plane. This is a plane with an upsidedown "V" cut into the bottom that can take different-shaped planing edges, which in turn, produce differently shaped bevels. You can still pick them up, but most people use a router.

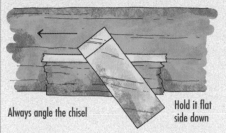

Fig. 9. *Hold an ordinary chisel like this to stop it digging into the wood.*

Always angle the chisel

Hold it flat side down

Carving is a subtle skill that takes time to acquire. If you're serious about it, you should consider taking some kind of class or at least picking up a dedicated how-to book. To carve even the simplest design in wood you'll need a selection of gouges and chisels, probably something like three gouges (deep, shallow and V-shaped) and three chisels (straight, bent and skew). Add to that a bench knife for shaving and rounding edges and you've got a usable beginner's carving kit. Carving's a wonderfully relaxing shift of pace from most shed work. It's quiet, slow and satisfying.

Turning is a good way to decorate many household woodworking projects, particularly those with legs and handles. It involves rotating the wood you want to work on while you hold the cutting tool still and then gently push it into the spinning wood. That means you need a lathe. Woodturning lathes are relatively expensive, so we've included a homemade version on pages 92–4 that will save you money. You'll need to bore a hole in each end of the wood to mount it on the lathe, and after that work the pedal with your foot to spin the wood. Although you can buy special chisels for lathe work, you can also start with an ordinary chisel or a gouge.

Fig. 8. *An old-fashioned plane for making bevels.*

⑥ JOINTS AND HOW TO MAKE THEM

While many of the projects in this book feature joints that require nothing more complicated than nailing and gluing, you will from time to time need to make stronger or just more attractive joints. On these pages you'll find some of the most common kinds.

Dowelled butt joint This is a simple way to add strength to a right-angled joint. Drill holes in both pieces of wood (on the side where they join) and then fit dowels—little wooden pins—into the holes. The only problem you're likely to encounter with a dowelled butt joint is making sure the holes line up correctly, so take your time and measure them accurately. Alternatively, if you can find some very small metal ball bearings, you can tape these to one of the pieces of wood in the correct position and then tap them with a wooden mallet so they dent the wood. Then, positioning the second piece of wood over the ball bearings, give it a couple of smart taps. When you separate the two pieces of wood, the indents will show you where the holes should go, and you can drill them out.

Fig. 10. *The dowelled butt joint is both simple and strong.*

Rabbet joint This is an excellent joint for making corners because the two pieces of wood can be glued, nailed or screwed on two surfaces. One piece of wood is simply cut square at the end, while the other has a notch cut into it (this should be the same size as the end of the first piece).

Fig. 11. *Lap joints are good for cross pieces and "T" joints.*

Lap or Lapped joint Made by cutting notches that are exactly the same size halfway into both pieces of wood that go to make the joint. Useful for right angles, crosspieces and "T" shapes. Make lap joints with a tenon saw— mark the width of the notch and then saw down halfway into the wood. Then use the saw to make further cuts between the edges of the joint so you can chisel it out. (See Fig. 11.)

Stopped joint Variously called a stopped housing or stopped dado joint, this is an excellent joint to use for shelves because you can hide the actual joint from sight. Taking a bookcase as an example, what you want to do is cut a shelf-sized groove into the walls of the bookcase so that you can slide the shelves into them. So, using the width of the shelf as your guide, mark the wall with a groove that stops about 1/2 in. (13 mm) from the edge and then saw and chisel this out. Cut a notch in the shelf of the same size (i.e., the depth of the groove multiplied by the distance from the edge) and the two will slot together. (The version that doesn't stop before the edge is called a "through" housing or dado joint. It's just as effective, but not as neat.)

Dovetail joint A bit of a woodworking classic, this is a very strong joint, consisting of interlocking "fingers" of wood (supposedly shaped like a dove's tail—hence the name), that comes in different varieties. There's a sliding version almost identical to the through-stopped joint (a through dovetail) which you'll often see on drawer corners, and a half-blind version where one side of the dovetail is hidden from view. These days, the way to make good dovetails is to use a special dovetailing jig and a router. You can make a dovetail joint by hand, however, using a little right-angled metal template which fits over the end of the piece of wood you're using to make the "tails"—mark round the template and then cut it out with a tenon saw. Then, you can use the tails as the template for the other part of the joint on the second piece of wood, the "pin." (See Fig. 12.)

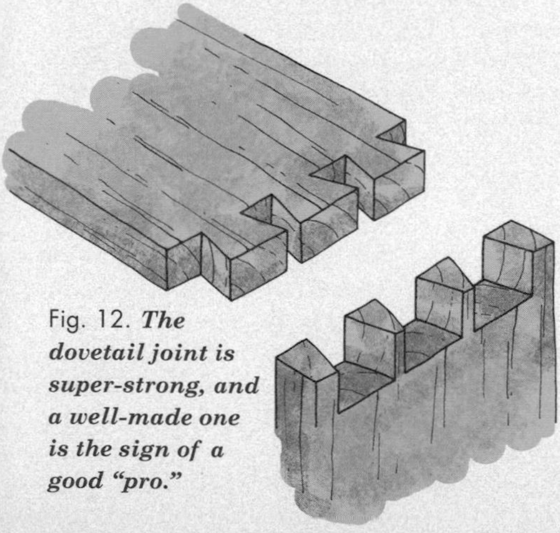

Mortise-and-tenon joint One of the strongest joints you can make, this is made up of one piece of wood with a recess cut into it (the mortise), and another with a "tongue" that fits exactly into the mortise. To make one by hand you'll need a mortise gauge, and a measuring device with two pins in it (which is used to score out the shape of the mortise on the first piece of wood). This is then hacked out with a chisel and a wooden mallet. You can use the gauge to mark out the correct size of the tenon and then cut this with a—surprise—tenon saw.

Fig. 13. *Mortise-and-tenon joints require careful measuring, and practice, in order to get a good fit.*

Fig. 12. *The dovetail joint is super-strong, and a well-made one is the sign of a good "pro."*

⑦ DECORATING WOOD

Wood, especially reclaimed wood, is beautiful in itself, but sometimes even nature needs a hand. And although modern wood can have its moments, too often it can look a bit sorry for itself and really benefits from some straightforward decoration or finishing off.

The simplest—and one of the most effective—ways to finish a job is to give it a topcoat, usually of shellac or varnish. (Some people love oil and wax, but we're not covering those here.) Shellac is actually made from beetle resin and is non-toxic and fast-drying. Although you can buy it in flakes and mix it yourself, buy ready-made to start with. Use a natural-bristle brush, and apply lightly in the direction of the wood grain to avoid bubbles and lines; and don't hang about, because shellac dries very rapidly. Use as many coats as you need to achieve the finish you want, allowing each one to dry thoroughly before applying the next one. In between each coat, rub down the surface with sandpaper, followed by fine steel wool, which is good for polishing and cleaning delicate surfaces. Shellac isn't waterproof, so you'll need to apply another coat on top—usually varnish.

Varnish has the advantage of being waterproof and the disadvantage of being toxic, smelly and messy. One solution is to use a water-based varnish, though you'll find that the finish isn't as long-lasting. Varnish goes on easy—just leave each coat overnight to dry and then give it a rub down with sandpaper. When you're done, use fine steel wool to get a perfect finish.

Painting wood works well, too—and not just in the "splash it all over" sense. One easy but highly effective option is an ebony stain, as used for the door fingerplate in Fig. 15. Sand the surface and the edges smooth in the direction of the grain and then mix some brightly colored oil paint with a bit of transparent varnish. Paint the design directly onto the wood (or use a stencil if you prefer) and then when it's pretty much dry, cover the whole thing with ebony stain—yes, even the paint. When the stain has sunk into the wood, rub it with a soft rag and watch what happens. The colored design will stand out beautifully on the black background. You'll find a wide range of stains and pigments in the stores—go for water-based ones, because they produce good results and aren't as messy to use.

As well as applying an attractive finish to wood, you can actually decorate it with fretwork (sometimes called latticework), which is a way of cutting out shapes inside a piece of wood. This is often added to a piece of work as an overlay, in which case the wood should be only 1/8 in. or 1/16 in. (3 or 1.5 mm) thick. For larger pieces like bookcases or cabinets, you can expect to be able to work with board that's up to 3/4 in. (19 mm) thick.

As you can guess, working with wood that's only 1/16 in. (1.5 mm) thick is tricky, so your best bet is to pin it to another piece of wood and cut through both of them. The usual tool for this is a fretsaw or keyhole saw, though you can buy electric scroll saws, which look a bit like sewing machines and make the work a lot easier!

Preparing for inlay | The finished piece

Fig. 14. *Inlaying can lift the look of an otherwise ordinary job.*

Although you can design fretwork patterns yourself, there are many companies that sell pre-drawn designs. These can be copied onto the wood, and produce first-class results.

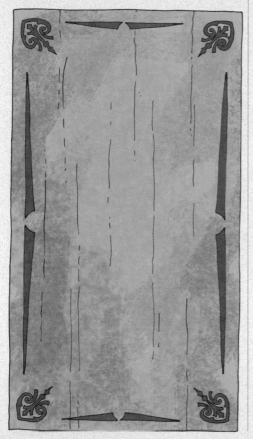

A door fingerplate

Fig. 15. *Painting a design onto wood and then staining it to a finish is one of the easiest and most effective ways to improve the look of your woodwork.*

Another interesting technique is inlaying. This involves fixing a thin layer of wood inside a thicker layer to form a pattern or motif. The two woods are usually chosen for their different colors (or they can be stained differently) or because they have very different grain characteristics. The idea is to draw a design on paper—simple geometric designs are a good place to start—and then cut the inlay wood to the correct shape but slightly oversize. You can then use a shooting board to plane all the edges square before gluing the shapes onto the paper. When the glue's set, you can ease off the paper with a knife and carefully add a very slight bevel to the inside. Place the design on the piece of wood that's going to take the inlay, and draw round it. Mark the shape with a very sharp knife and then use a chisel to cut across the grain—see Fig. 14. Chisel to within about 1/16 in. (1.5 mm) of the outer edge of the shape, then turn the chisel bevel side down and remove the wood to the depth of the inlay. You can then fit and glue the inlay into position.

17

(8) SOLDERING

In principle, soldering is a simple job—it's just a way of joining together two or more metals using an alloy that has a relatively low melting point; the alloy "glues" the other bits of metal together. In practice, it's more complex, and soldering requires exactly that—practice.

The process involves two main components—the solder and the soldering iron. The iron generates the heat required to melt the solder; a soldering iron rated between 15 and 30W is sufficient for all your hobby jobs. Thin solder works best (1/30 in., or 0.75 mm) and you should try to buy what's called rosin-core solder for electronics work, with a rating of 60/40—that's 60 percent tin and 40 percent lead.

Before you solder, make sure that all the surfaces involved in the job are clean. A light brushing with steel wool usually does the trick. Next, the tip of the iron needs to be "tinned"—given a little jacket of solder—and then wiped away with a damp sponge. This simple bit of preparation improves the thermal contact between the iron and the thing you're trying to solder.

You'll usually get better results if you can secure what you're working on in some way, and then start by heating everything that goes to make up the joint to the same

Thin solder
works best

temperature before you apply the solder. That way it will run over the joint more easily. Heat the joint with the tip of the iron and then keep it hot while you apply the solder. Remove the iron and let the joint cool. Keep a careful eye on the amount of solder you're using—too much can cause electronic circuit boards to short, too little and the joint won't be secure. Experience and practice are your best guides here.

You should make sure that you solder in an area that's well-ventilated (because solder gives off unpleasant fumes), and wear some kind of eye protection. Finally, treat solder with respect—even a small splash will give you a nasty burn.

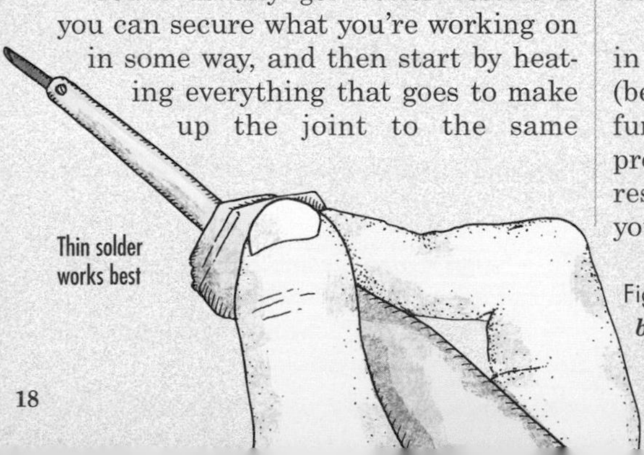

Fig. 16. *Soldering irons should be "tinned" and wiped clean before use.*

9 USEFUL KNOTS

Although most of the projects here rely on permanent fixing using glue, nails or screws, it's also good to know your way around a few knots. These can be useful for specific projects—like the rope ladder and rope swing on page 69—but also for temporarily securing one thing to another.

There are different kinds of knots. Some are designed to secure an object from the start while others grow tighter under pressure; some slide, and others are specifically tied so that you can undo them quickly. You should inspect any rope—particularly if it's designed to be weight-bearing—regularly for wear and tear, and store it in loops out of direct sunlight. If you're using synthetic rope it's a good idea to wrap the part you're going to cut with gaffer tape and then cut it. After that, burn the ends with a match—this will fuse them together and stop them from unravelling.

Here are four useful knots:

Fig. 17—The Clove Hitch
An excellent way to attach a line to a pole, ring or peg, this is the knot needed to make the rope ladder on page 69. It's also called the Peg Knot or Boatmen's Knot because of its popularity at sea.

Fig. 18—The Sheet-Bend Knot
This is the best knot for tying two unequal-sized lengths of rope together. It's very secure and will also work with cord made from different materials— i.e., string and nylon rope. Sailors use it for tying down sails.

Fig. 19—Figure-of-Eight Knot
This is mainly used to make a good stopper when you've passed a length of cord through a hole in something and need to secure it on the other side. If you double it over, it'll also provide a strong loop at the end of the line.

Fig. 20—The Round Turn and Two Half Hitches
This strong and easy-to-tie knot is one of the best and most secure ways to tie a rope to a tree or a pole. Use it to secure both the rope ladder and swing described on page 69. It almost never jams and, with practice, is quick to tie.

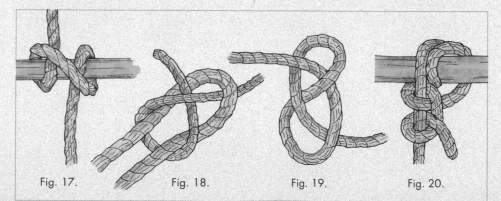

Fig. 17.   Fig. 18.   Fig. 19.   Fig. 20.

10 CARING FOR TOOLS

Even modern tools need looking after, and if you take the trouble, they'll give you many years of reliable service.

A sharp tool shouldn't need much force to do its job, so if you find you're having to work too hard, then you need to look at the blade. Grind chisels and plane blades on an abrasive wheel to a 25-degree angle—dip them in water as you do this and work the blades back and forth along the wheel to ensure even wear. Oilstones are still the best way to shape the cutting edge—to a 30-degree angle—by pushing the blade away from you with steady strokes down the length of the stone. Get a honing guide for this—it's an inexpensive gizmo that will help you get the angle right. At the end, you'll have a little burr on the edge of the tool, so flip it and then make a single stroke down the stone to remove it.

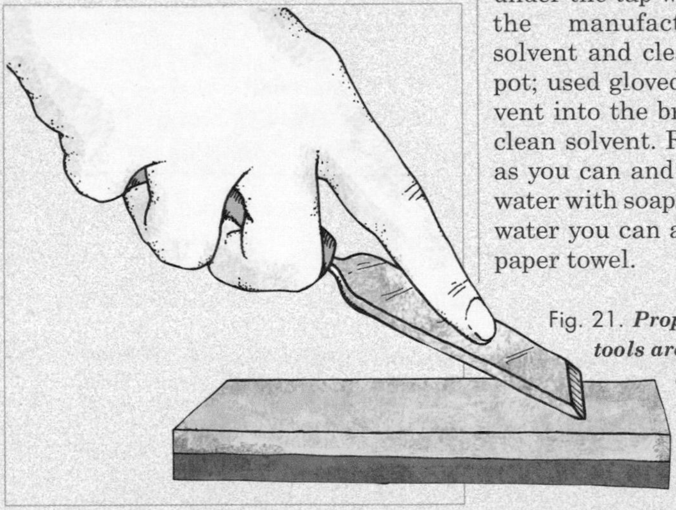

Sharpening saws is a pain. Put them in a vice, teeth facing up, and use a round file to sharpen each tooth—the side with the bevel as opposed to the straight side—on both sides of the saw. Wear gloves. Drill bits can be kept sharp with a grindstone.

Tools left on the floor are more likely to rust, so hang them on the wall—you can paint their shape behind them if you like—and keep the small stuff in a cupboard or toolbox. Follow manufacturer's instructions for cleaning after use and remember that a light coat of oil on metal surfaces will prevent rust.

Some things, like glue, have a limited shelf life and won't be at their best beyond that point. They're usually inexpensive, so it pays to keep on top of things and replace when necessary. Clean your brushes after each session, too. If you've been using them to apply anything that's water-based, just rinse under the tap with soap. Otherwise, get the manufacturer's recommended solvent and clean the brush in a little pot; used gloved hands to work the solvent into the bristles, then repeat with clean solvent. Remove as much solvent as you can and then wash under warm water with soap. Get rid of all the excess water you can and wrap the brush in a paper towel.

Fig. 21. *Properly sharpened tools are more accurate and easier to use.*

⑪ SAFETY

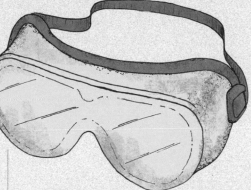

Accidents are a part of life that's best avoided, and, as nearly all of the projects in this book involve things that cut or scrape or bore holes, it's worth reviewing some basic safety tips. This way the cuts, scrapes and holes end up in the wood or metal, where they're supposed to be, rather than in you.

Your brain is sharper than any knife and more powerful than any drill, so make sure you use it. Thinking about what you're going to do before you actually do it is the best way to avoid accidents and mistakes, so concentrate on what you're doing and don't stop until you've finished—many saw cuts, for example, happen because you take your eyes off the blade before you've actually finished cutting. Don't rush things—you're probably not on a deadline, and this is supposed to be fun—and never work when you're tired.

A tidy shed may sound like a misnomer, but keeping things squared away means you'll not only be able to find what you need more quickly, you're also less likely to trip or knock things over. Unless there's a good reason not to, you should pack your tools away at the end of every session; assuming they're sharp—which they should be—you don't want to leave them lying around.

While we're on the subject, wear proper clothing and protect yourself if you need to—goggles for when you're drilling (especially through metal), earplugs if you're using power tools in a confined space, and a mask if you're generating a lot of dust or using chemicals. Make sure your shed is properly

Fig. 22. Some safety tips—like wearing goggles when drilling—are obvious. Others are less so, but all are important and should never be ignored.

ventilated, too—at least keep the door open if you're applying weatherproofing or using a lot of glue. Remember that loose clothing can get caught in power tools and so can jewelry; and if you've got long hair, tie it back.

Finally, your shed should be equipped with both a small fire extinguisher and a first-aid kit—and make sure you know how to use them. One last point: if you've had a drink or are taking medication, just relax and watch television instead.

Instructions are usually included for a reason, and although it may be tempting to just fire up your latest electric-powered monster and get cracking, you should resist this until you've had a chance to review its safety features. It's also useful to find a place in your shed to store manuals and how-to books so that they're on hand when you need them; you won't put yourself in danger because you can only vaguely remember how something works.

(12) STAND FOR A MODEL YACHT

Unless you want to take down their sails and rigging every time, model yachts are hard to store. This easy-to-build stand lets you provide your favorite model boat with a permanent berth on your desk.

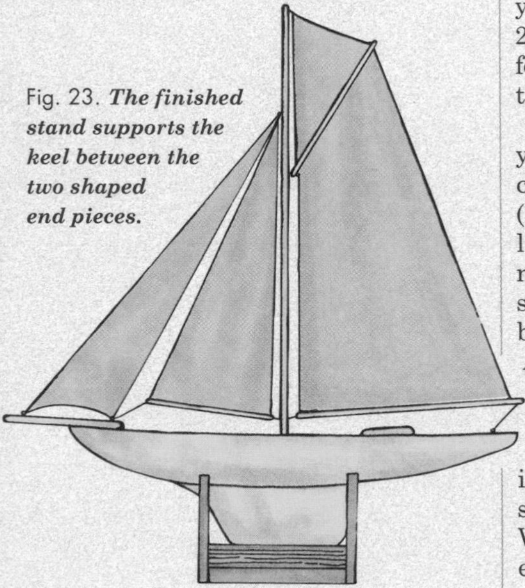

Fig. 23. *The finished stand supports the keel between the two shaped end pieces.*

Since yachts vary so much in size, there's no point in giving you any measurements, but you'll need some three-ply plywood for the ends and some pine for the base and keel holder. The ply needs to be as wide as the widest part of the deck and deep enough that, when the boat is on the stand, the actual keel is about 1/2 in. (123 mm) from the bottom edge.

Use a fretsaw to cut out the curved portion for each end of the stand—this will inevitably require a bit of movement back and forth until you achieve the correct curve. Remember to cut an appropriate-sized slot into the three-ply to accommodate the front and end sections of the keel.

Now you need to measure the length of the keel at a point about 1 in. (25 mm) down from the hull. That's the length of your base. Finally, cut two pieces of 2 x 1/2 in. (51 x 13 mm) pine as a "seat" for the keel, making sure they're exactly the same length as the base.

To fit the five pieces of wood together you'll need some wood glue and ten countersunk screws of about 1 in. (25 mm) long. Glue and screw the two lengths of pine to the base on their narrow edges as shown in Fig. 24. They should be far enough apart so that the bottom of the keel fits between them. Attach them with the countersunk screws from beneath the base and then screw on the two ends in the same way.

To finish up, get some old felt or similar thick, soft cloth and glue a narrow strip to the top surface of the two ends. When it's set, you can snip off the excess and you have a gentle cradle that won't harm the bow of your ship.

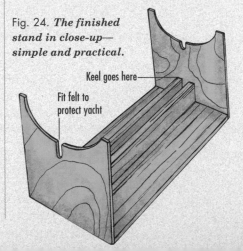

Fig. 24. *The finished stand in close-up— simple and practical.*

Keel goes here

Fit felt to protect yacht

13 PULSE RECORDER

Although you probably won't find one at your local doctor's office, this is nevertheless an interesting experiment that will show someone's pulse rate. You'll need a large cork, a coat button (the kind that has a metal ring on the back), some flexible wire, a drawing pin, a match with the striking end removed, a small quill with the feathers removed and a piece of card with one side blackened by the flame of a candle.

To use the pulse recorder, place the blackened side of the card against the quill as in the picture. Get a friend to rest their wrist gently on top of the button. As soon as they're in position, start to pull the card away from the cork, making sure you keep it in contact with the quill. As each beat is felt, the quill makes a thin white line on the blackened card; in between each beat, the button and the quill will lift again. As you pull the card away from the cork, you'll end up with a series of jagged lines—a regular pattern indicates a healthy pulse.

Blackened card — Coat button

Flexible wire

Fig. 25. *Side view of the finished pulse recorder in action.*

Cut a mortise right through one end of the cork. The hole needs to be big enough to allow the match to move freely up and down. Press the button into the top of the cork so that the ring sits neatly in the mortise, then push the match into the mortise and into the button ring.

Loop one end of the wire round the drawing pin and then push the pin into the bottom of the cork. Take the other end of the wire and thread it through the button ring so it fits snugly next to the match. Once you've tried this, you can trim the wire to the correct length.

Cut a small slit in the end of the match with a penknife and insert the quill. A small blob of melted candle wax or fine twine should secure it (you may find it easier to remove the match from the cork for this bit). And that's it.

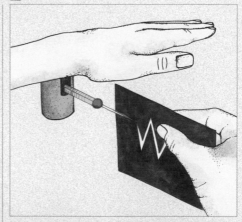

Fig. 26. *As you move the card away from the recorder, the pulse from the left hand will "bounce" the quill and scratch a pattern on it.*

14 PICTURE FRAMES

Although it's possible to make your own mouldings from scratch, these days off-the-shelf ones are so good and easy to obtain that it's not really worth it. It also saves loads of time.

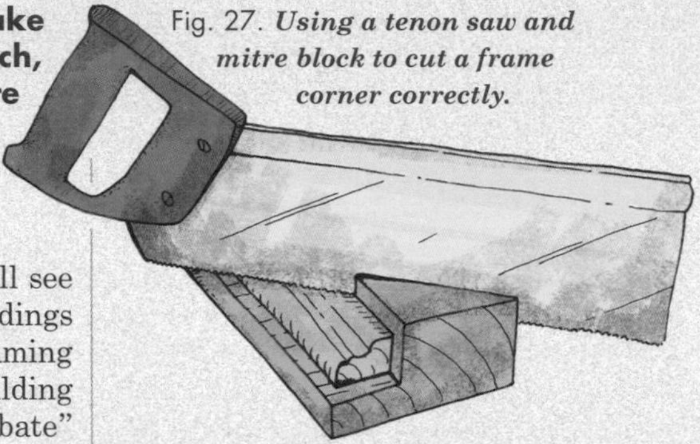

Fig. 27. *Using a tenon saw and mitre block to cut a frame corner correctly.*

If you have a look at Fig. 28 you'll see four typical picture-frame mouldings (which could also be used for framing small mirrors). Each type of moulding comes with what's called a "rebate" already cut into it—this is simply a lip that runs the length of the wood, and that actually holds the glass in place over the picture. Because mouldings are already decorated and shaped to take a picture, all you have to do is decide on the style and then cut them to size. This is best done using a miter block (as shown in Fig. 27), which is designed to allow you to cut wood at exactly 45 degrees. Alternatively, if you plan to make lots of angled cuts for different projects, you can buy an adjustable mitre saw, which will handle many different angles accurately.

What you have to remember is that the size of the frame you need is based on the size of the picture, plus the width of the frame itself. So, if you have a photograph or certificate that's 12 x 9 in. (304 x 228 mm) and your frame moulding is 1 1/2 in. (38 mm) wide, then you'll actually need to add 3 in. (76 mm) to the length of each piece, meaning that you end up with two long sides measuring 15 in. (381 mm) and two short sides of 12 in. (304 mm).

If you're using a miter block, then you need to hold the moulding as tight as you can to the inside edge of the block, with the moulding facing you.

Then you slip the tenon saw into the precut groove in the mitre block and start to saw. When you've made the first cut, mark the length of the picture on the upper edge of the rebate—add 1/16 in. (2 mm) clearance—and then you can line this up with the precut angle in the miter block. Now you can make the second cut to the wood to complete one side of the frame.

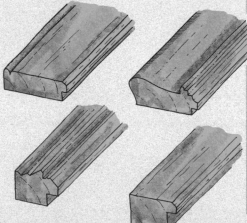

Fig. 28. *Four typical mouldings. The one at the bottom right is mainly used for prints and photographs.*

Of course, your frames are going to fit perfectly when cut, but, if they don't, you'll need to make yourself something called a "shooting board," which will help you with this and many other projects. Start with a length of wood 24 x 6 x 1 in. (610 x 152 x 25 mm). Get three smaller pieces 9 x 2 x 1 in. (228 x 51 x 25 mm) and screw them crossways onto the first piece at right angles, so each one sticks out by 3 in. (76 mm). Get a second strip of wood 24 x 2³/4 x ¹/2 in. (610 x 70 x 13 mm) and screw it onto the three projecting strips, flush to their ends—this will leave a ¹/4 in. (6 mm) gap into which your plane can slide along on its side. The final piece is a length of wood 2 in. (51 mm) wide and ³/4 in. (19 mm), thick and long enough so that it fits across at an angle of precisely 45 degrees. Obviously, it's crucial that this angle is accurate, so set it with a compass before angling the ends of the wood and screwing it in place. (Alternatively, a mitre box is already set up to cut 45- and 90-degree angles.)

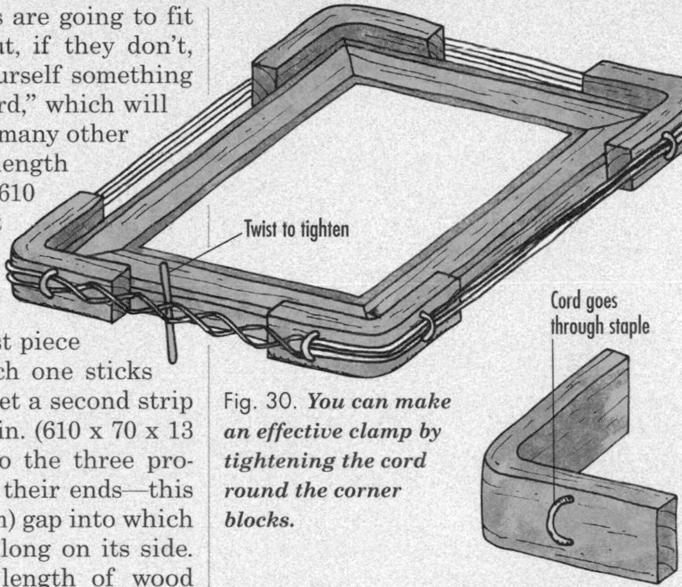

Twist to tighten

Cord goes through staple

Fig. 30. *You can make an effective clamp by tightening the cord round the corner blocks.*

Fig. 29. *Use a shooting board to plane off a very fine shaving.*

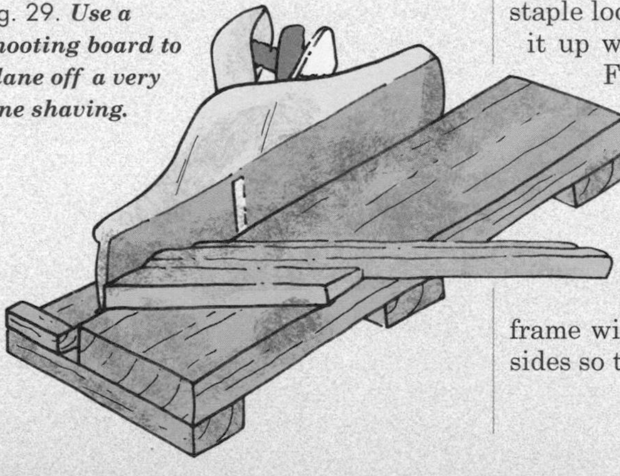

Having mitred the ends of the frame so that they fit perfectly, you need to glue them together. You can buy a mitre clamp for this, but, if you only need it occasionally, it's cheaper to make some hardwood corners yourself. They just need to be pure right angles on the inside with one heavy-duty staple on each outside edge. Then, when the frame is glued, you put one on each corner and run string through each of the staple loops, all the way round. Tighten it up with a short stick as shown in Fig. 30. If it still doesn't feel secure when the glue has dried, bang a small nail into each corner.

Finish the frame with a sheet of glass, the picture and then a piece of ¹/8 in. (4 mm) wood, sized to fit. Secure the frame with small nails banged into the sides so they hold the back in place.

⑮ SHIP IN A BOTTLE

This is a classic "trick" that still has people scratching their heads, yet the solution is simplicity itself. The trick is to find a bottle with a slightly larger-than-average neck. You'll need a model sailing ship of the kind with masts and sails. In order to get the ship into the bottle, it's necessary to hinge the masts away from the bow, so that they can be pushed flat. That's how you get the ship into the bottle.

If you're skilled at model-making, you can buy tiny hinges that will do the job, but it's very fussy. Instead, try gluing a tiny strip of leather behind each mast to act as a hinge. That way, when you cut through the masts with a sharp knife, you can push them backwards—toward the stern—and then put the boat inside the bottle.

How do you raise the masts? Simple. Make tiny holes in the masts and cross-pieces and thread cotton or fine fishing line through them. Then, after you've pushed the boat into the bottle, you can pull on the line and lift the masts back up again. Then cut the line and no one will be any the wiser.

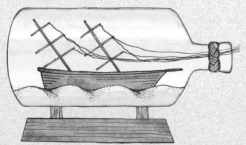

⑯ HOOP-THROWING GAME

All you need for this fairground-style game is a piece of wood, some rubber rings of the kind used to seal large pickle or jam jars, some screw hooks and a way of putting numbers onto the wood so that players know how much they've scored.

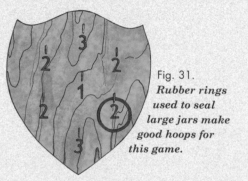

Fig. 31.
Rubber rings used to seal large jars make good hoops for this game.

A piece of hardwood about 12 in. (305 mm) square will do fine for the back. Draw a nice shape onto the board—a circle, clover or shield shape works well—and then saw round it, finishing off any rough edges with sandpaper. Screw in the hooks in any arrangement you fancy and then add the numbers. You can either write these on yourself or use the sticky-backed kind that you can buy from good hardware stores—they're not expensive.

When you've positioned both the hooks and the numbers, take the hooks out again and give the board a few coats of varnish. When it's completely dry, screw the hooks back in. You play the game by throwing the rubber rings against the board and trying to land on the hook with the biggest number.

⑰ SERVING TRAY

This is a nice easy job that you can do in a couple of hours. Use any fancy hardwood for the sides and handles if you can scrounge it up, otherwise pine will do fine.

The two sides are 21 x 1³/₄ x ¹/₂ in. (533 x 44.5 x 13 mm); the handle ends are 11¹/₂ x 3 x ¹/₂ in. (292 x 76 x 13 mm) and the bottom is 20¹/₂ x 11¹/₂ x ¹/₂ in. (521 x 292 x 13 mm) and can be made from ordinary plywood. (Cut this when you've prepared the sides and handles so that you can make sure it fits exactly).

The diagram below shows the plan for the handles at either end. Draw out the rounded shape on your wood—the two ends must be the same height as your sides (1³/₄ in. or 44.5 mm) and then saw it out. When you've got it roughly right, mark out where the handle hole goes in relation—the more closely it mirrors the curve of the top the neater it will look—and then drill out two finger-sized holes on either end. Drill out the gap in between and finish with a chisel or fretsaw and use this as the template for the other handle.

You need to mark and then gouge a ¹/₂ in. (13 mm) wide and ¹/₄ in. (6 mm) deep right-angled slot around the bottom of the inside edges of both sides and ends—this is to take the plywood

bottom of the tray. Use sandpaper to smooth and round any rough edges off the sides and handles and then glue and tack the sides and handles together. When the glue has dried, fit the plywood bottom into the frame, making any adjustments necessary to ensure it's snug. Glue and tack it in place. Finally, use finishing nails to secure the sides, handle ends and bottom together. Stain to finish.

Fig. 32. *This simple tray is perfect for breakfast in bed (or in the shed).*

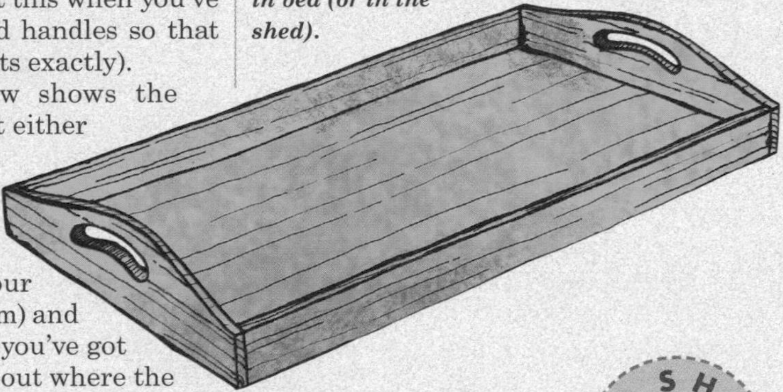

1 ³/₄ in (44.5 mm)

11 ¹/₂ in (292 mm)

The Coldest Shed

There's an infamous shed in Nederland, Colorado, that holds a grisly secret—though it's no longer much of a secret since being reported all over the world and, more recently, turned into a film. This is the chilling story of Bredo Morstoel, who was frozen solid by his grandson in 1983 as a cut-price experiment in cryogenics. He's still there in the shed, biding his time under a large pile of dry ice...

⑱ ELECTRIC MODEL-RAILROAD SIGNAL

If you're a model-railroad fan who's into retro styling, this old-fashioned signal will help keep everything running on time.

The signal pole is made from a 9 in. (228 mm) piece of wood that is 5/16 in. (8 mm) square at the bottom, tapering to 1/4 in. (6 mm) at the top. You can make the arm from a piece of balsa. This should be 21/8 in. (54 mm) long and 5/16 in. (8 mm) wide—except at the tail end, where it should be twice that. Balsa is easy to work with and you can just round it off to the shape shown here. Make a pinhole in the tail end and another hole in the main arm as shown. Secure the arm to the pole with a small flat-head nail, but make sure there's plenty of "play," as the arm must be able to move up and down freely. Finally, put a tiny pin into the pole above the arm so it can't go beyond the horizontal.

For the electrical bit you need a 11/8 in. (30 mm) tube of brass or copper with a bore of 1/8 in. (3 mm) covered with two or three layers of gummed paper. Next you need some 30 SWG (Standard Wire Gauge) cotton- or silk-covered wire. Lay one end along the tube, leaving about 11/2 in. (38 mm) sticking out, and then wind the wire round the tube. Do this six times, making sure the first layer is wrapped tightly, and finish with a light twist or two around the spare wire end to stop it coming uncoiled.

Make a paper tube large enough to slip the coil inside and then carefully fill the inside with melted candle wax, taking care to keep the inside of the metal tube completely clear. Then fix the coil to the pole with gummed paper.

Use some sturdy 16 SWG wire to create a hook with a 5/8 in. (16 mm) shank and a weight—this is bent into a small circle and has a hook on one end. Connect the shank of the hook to the hole in the signal arm with cotton, so that when the arm is straight you've got about 1/8 in. (3 mm) of shank inside the coil. When you connect the two wires to a battery, the magnetism inside the coil will "pull" the shank and hook up inside the tube and make the signal fall. Disconnect the battery and the weight will pull the signal straight again.

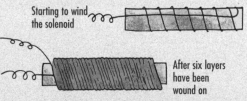

Starting to wind the solenoid

After six layers have been wound on

Fig. 33. *The finished railroad signal with everything attached. The signal arm has been set to "danger."*

19 KALEIDOSCOPE

Kaleidoscopes are a classic toy of yesteryear, and this simple version will give you hours of fun.

Fig. 34. *The basis of this project is three pieces of ordinary window glass.*

Secure with tape when painted

You'll need a sheet of stiff card of about 12 x 7½ in. (305 x 190 mm) for the tube. Bend it into a tube so the edges overlap a bit and get a friend to tie some string round each end to hold it together. Either glue the card directly or glue a strip of strong paper down the length of the join between the bits of string. When it's set, remove the string and add two more strips of paper to complete the seal.

You now need three strips of plain window glass about 11½ x 2 in. (292 x 51 mm) and two circles of glass the same circumference as the tube; one of these needs to be "obscured" glass (glass that's been etched or similarly treated so that visibility is impaired). Because the strips are going to be stuck together in a long triangle to make a reflector, do a dummy first from cardboard to make sure it'll fit in the tube. Then get the glass, paint one side of each piece with thick black paint and let it dry. Fit them together into a triangle— painted sides out—using gaffer tape, and then slide them into the cardboard tube. Use more tape if necessary to get a snug fit.

Cut a circle of cardboard about ¼ in. (6 mm) bigger all round than the circumference of the kaleidoscope and cut an eyehole in its center ½ in. (13 mm) in diameter. Make four ¼ in. (6 mm) cuts around the edge of the circle and fold the edges up—this will give you a flat edge that you can glue to the inside at one end of the tube.

When that's set, turn the tube so that the eyehole is on the bottom and pop the first circle of glass in the open end. It will rest on the glass pyramid inside. Cut a strip of card long enough to fit into the end of the tube when bent into a circle—it should be narrow enough to leave room for the piece of obscured glass to sit on top of it, flush with the end of the tube. Fill the space between the first circle of glass and the end about two-thirds full of broken colored glass and colored beads—nothing bigger than ¼ in. (6 mm) across—and then tape the obscured glass to the top. To use your kaleidoscope, hold it up to the light, and slowly rotate the tube.

Broken beads and glass

Obscured glass circle

Circle of clear glass

20 BOX CART

This is a more sophisticated version of the traditional go-kart that allows you to propel yourself forward by means of a clever vertical control lever and crankshaft combo.

To make it you'll need five pieces of 36 x 2 x 1/2 in. (914 x 51 x 13 mm) batten, a packing case for the seat, a load of 1 1/2 in. (38 mm) wire nails, four wheels, twelve washers, some large round staples, two bolts, and two iron bars for the axles. Since the back axle needs to be bent to make the crank, and both axles need holes drilled in each end to help secure the wheels, you'll need a friendly local hardware store or a little sheet-

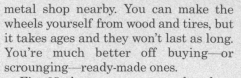

metal shop nearby. You can make the wheels yourself from wood and tires, but it takes ages and they won't last as long. You're much better off buying—or scrounging—ready-made ones.

Fig. 35 shows you more or less how the thing goes together. Nail two of the 36 in. (914 mm) battens to a smaller 9 in. (229 mm) length to form the front and sides. The front piece needs to have a notch cut into it so that you can fit a second, 10 in. (254 mm) long piece of batten into it, to form a "T" shape. At the bottom of the "T" you'll also fit another piece of wood across the frame, but you don't need to think about that just yet.

Make the seat out of pack-ing-case wood. The back-plate is 24 x 18 in. (610 x 457 mm) and doesn't need to be a single, complete piece of wood. The sides of the seat are 12 in. (305 mm) square and the seat is 18 x 12 in. (457 x 305 mm). Nail the seat and back together and to the frame as shown in Fig. 35 using the 1 1/2 in. (38 mm) wire nails.

The seat

Driving lever

The footrest

Front axle

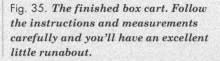

Fig. 35. *The finished box cart. Follow the instructions and measurements carefully and you'll have an excellent little runabout.*

You'll need a strong piece of planking 8 in. (203 mm) wide to secure the driving lever in the middle of the cart. Nail this into place on the side battens, as shown, 6 in. (152 mm) away from the seat, and then trim off the sides to the correct angle and sand them down. You can now measure, cut and fit the remaining crosspiece to the side battens (this connects to the bottom end of the "T").

The axle batten (Fig. 36) should be 22 in. (559 mm) long, and you'll need to bore a hole in the center for the steering bolt. Five large U-shaped staples are enough to attach the axle to the batten—make sure there's enough play so that it revolves!—and then you can slip on the wheels, securing them with a cotter pin at each end. You can make the footrests from any old bits of batten you've got left over and then just nail them to the steering crosspiece. Secure the front axle to the main frame with a bolt and washer and make sure there's

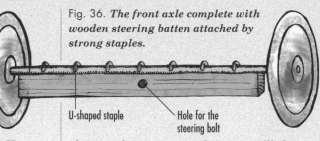

Fig. 36. *The front axle complete with wooden steering batten attached by strong staples.*

U-shaped staple   Hole for the steering bolt

plenty of movement there—you'll be steering this using your feet to push left and right on the front axle, so it needs to pivot properly.

Get your hardware store to put a 2 in. (51 mm) crank in the back axle, and then drill four holes in two pieces of batten. The rear ones need to be big enough to accommodate the axle and the front ones to accommodate the other bolt. When you've done that, thread the battens over the crank through the back holes. Place a piece of wood between the two battens (see Fig. 37) and then nail the three together; this will help to keep the crank stable—if it wobbles too much it'll be harder to use. Because the battens are all 1/2 in. (13 mm) wide, using three sandwiched together like this gives you 1/4 in. (6 mm) of "play" either side of the crank bend.

The main control lever is 24 in. (610 mm) long and will need a hole bored right through, near the top, to take a 12 in. (305 mm) rod of wood—that's your handlebars. At the lever end of the handle you'll need a bolt and washers to secure it to the parallel pieces of batten. Thread the bolt through the holes and pop on a washer. Screw a nut onto the bolt so it's close to the washer but still allows a little play, then screw on a second nut tight to the first and squeeze it onto the axle with a cycle wrench. The control lever needs to be

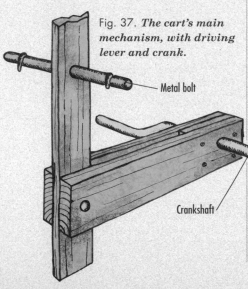

Fig. 37. *The cart's main mechanism, with driving lever and crank.*

— Metal bolt

Crankshaft

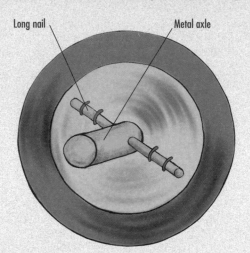

Long nail   Metal axle

Fig. 38. *The nail goes through the axle and is secured to the wheel by staples.*

attached to the front platform by means of an iron bar—so drill a hole through the lever, thread the bar through and then secure it with large staples (the same kind you used for the back axle).

Nearly there. Back at the rear axle, line everything up, drill a hole in each side batten for the axle, and then you can attach the wheels. The big difference between the front and rear wheel attachments is that the front wheels run free while the back ones have to turn with the axle—if they don't, you won't be able to drive the car along with the handle. The easiest way to fix the wheels to the back axle is shown in Fig. 38. Basically, you thread a strong nail through the hole at the end of the axle and then attach this to the wheel using strong staples, two on either side of the axle.

Oil all the moving parts and you're ready for the off. It takes some practice—and strong arms—to get this moving, but with a little practice you'll soon get the hang of it.

21 MAGIC PAPER RINGS

This conjuring trick demonstrates the unexpected effects that can be acheived by twisting strips of paper in different ways.

You'll need three lengths of ordinary paper, about 12 x 2 in. (305 x 51 mm). Mark a dotted line lengthwise down the center of each strip—a bit like the white lines on a road.

Take the first length and glue the ends together like a collar. Take the second strip and on this occasion introduce a single twist before you glue the end. Then take the third strip and twist it twice before gluing the ends together. Let the glue set and then cut carefully down the dotted lines on each of the rings.

The first ring will separate neatly in two. The second will form a single figure of eight, while the third becomes two rings linked together like a chain.

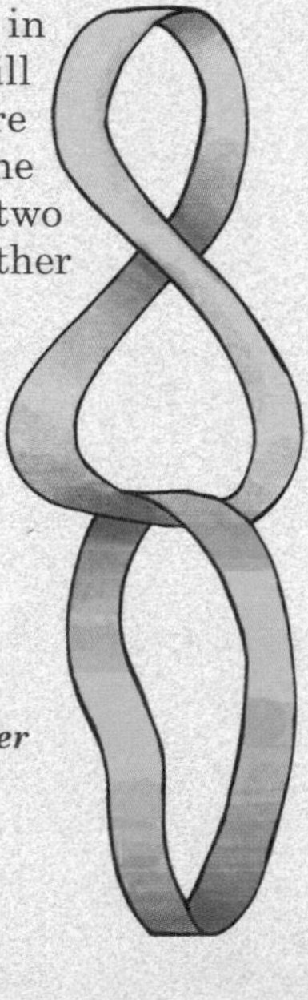

Fig. 39. *By cutting a twisted piece of paper ring along a dotted line, you'll produce the joined rings as shown here.*

㉒ THE TURNING TIGER

For this puzzle you'll need a couple of pieces of card, a sharp knife, scissors, some tracing paper and some slight artistic skill.

First, draw a line 1/2 in. (13 mm) down from the top and another the same distance from the bottom of the card. Fold along both lines. Next, draw out ten narrow panels on the front of the card, carefully score these with a knife and

Fig. 40. *Trace the tiger onto a piece of card exactly like this.*

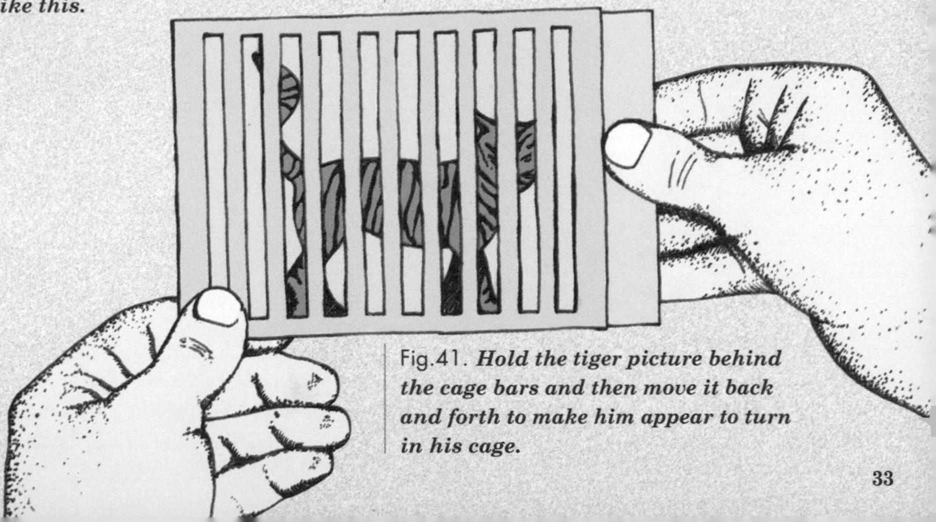

then cut them out with a pair of sharp scissors. You're now left with the bars of your "cage."

The second step is to take another piece of card and cut it so that it fits neatly behind the first and can be held in place at the top and bottom by the flaps. Next, trace or copy the strange design from Fig. 40—copy it exactly and, if you want it to have even more impact, color it in. The other thing you need to be careful of is that the vertical gaps in the picture are the same width as the bars on the first piece of card—otherwise the trick won't work.

Slide the picture behind the first piece of card and, holding one of the flaps marked on Fig. 40, move it back and forth behind the bars. As you do, you'll see the tiger flip from facing right to left and then back again. You needn't restrict yourself to tigers, either—with some thought and a little imagination, you can transform all sorts of interesting objects!

Fig. 41. *Hold the tiger picture behind the cage bars and then move it back and forth to make him appear to turn in his cage.*

㉓ FLAT KITE

Here's how to make a classic flat kite that's both strong and very easy to fly. In a stiff breeze you won't even have to run to launch this—it should rise at a 60-degree angle from the ground from a standing start.

Use straight-grained pine for the two central rods. These should be 45 1/2 x 1/2 x 5/16 in. (1156 x 13 x 8 mm) for the cross piece and 49 x 3/8 x 7/16 in. (1245 x 1 x 12 mm) for the vertical piece; to make the kite lighter (though less controllable) you could also consider using bamboo poles of the same dimensions.

Next you'll need to cut out some calico. Although it's tempting to use a single piece of cloth cut into the shape shown in Fig. 42, you're actually better off cutting out two separate pieces for the left and right sides of the main kite and a third for the keel (Fig. 43). That way you can make sure that the warp (the threads that run lengthwise in the fabric—see Fig. 42) is all pointing in the same direction. This will help to make your kite a good flyer.

Sew the two pieces of calico together and then add pockets of cloth in every corner to take the poles; these need to be about 4 in. (102 mm) deep. Once both the crosspiece and the vertical rod have been fitted into the pockets, bind the two rods together where they meet with string. Then measure down 5 1/2 in. (140 mm) from the top of the longest side of the calico you're using for the keel, and cut out a notch the width of the crosspiece. Line up the notch with the crosspiece, then fold the long edges above and below it around the vertical pole and sew them into position. Finally, sew on an extra piece of cloth at the keel corner—where you're going to attach the string.

Remember: Never fly your kite near power lines, roads or railways, airports (seriously!) or during a thunderstorm.

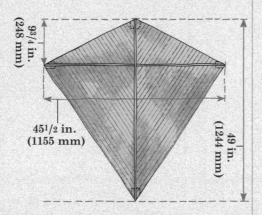

Fig.42. *This is a big, powerful kite that will fly well in strong winds.*

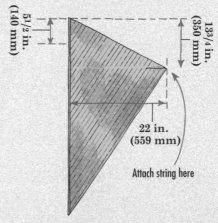

Fig.43. *The kite's keel – reinforce the corner where you attach the string with cloth.*

24 CYCLE SIREN

With a few bits and pieces you can make a surprisingly effective cycle siren that will leave other road users in no doubt that you're coming!

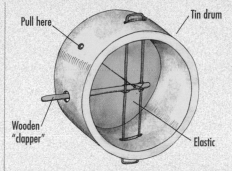

Get a shallow, round tin and take the lid off. Next get a piece of hardwood about half as long again as the diameter of the tin and 1/4 in. (6 mm) square. Drill a hole in the side of the tin so that the wood—we'll call it the "clapper"—fits loosely enough to allow it to vibrate. Next you need to attach a rubber band across the middle of the tin at right angles to the clapper. Make two holes, top and bottom, and thread the band through; pull it tight and tie it off (you may find it useful to fold a small piece of paper between the edges of the holes to stop the rubber band from fraying). Make sure that one length of the rubber band goes over the clapper and the other goes under it and then secure the band to the clapper with a short piece of wire.

Next, drill a small hole halfway between the clapper hole and the holes for the elastic bands. This should be big enough for a length of wire to pass through.

To attach the siren to the bike you'll need to get a friendly sheet-metal shop or hardware store to make up a strip of 1 in. (25 mm) tin plate that you can bend round the front-left fork of your bike and then pinch together at the ends—these need to stick out by about 1 in. (25 mm). Drill a hole through the ends and another into the tin and use a nut and bolt to fasten the two together.

Run a length of wire down from the handlebars through the remaining hole in the tin, and then secure it to the clapper. Now, by pulling on the wire, you'll force the end of the clapper out so that it touches the spokes of the wheel as they turn. The clapper will then vibrate on the "drum" of the tin and make quite a racket. You may need to experiment with the exact position of the tin/clapper/fixing so that the clapper doesn't actually get jammed in the spokes.

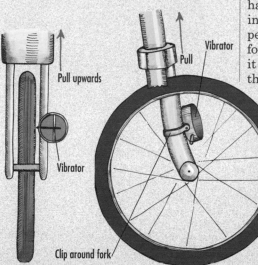

Fig. 44. Here's the siren attached to the front wheel of the bicycle— note that it attaches to the left fork.

25 GLYCERINE CORK PICTURE

This is a terrific little experiment that uses static electricity. All you'll need is a couple of hardback books, a sheet of glass, some cork filings, a little tub of glycerine and a torch.

Get two hardback books of the same size and place them on the table as shown in the picture. File a bottle cork to produce a pile of shavings and place them between the two books. Next take a sheet of ordinary glass and place it on top of the books so it forms a "bridge" over the cork shavings. Rub the top of the glass with some cloth (wool, silk or man-made fiber will work) and watch what happens—you'll see the cork shavings are attracted to the glass, rather like iron filings are to a magnet.

Now you've seen the principle, you can turn it into a trick. You'll need to rub some glycerine onto the glass in an interesting or funny shape— if you know the person you're trying to trick, you could even write their first name on the glass. Obviously, you need to do this before your friend arrives.

Make sure the room is dark and set up the books and cork shavings as before. Show your friend the "blank" glass—in the gloom they won't be able to see the glycerine marks. Then tell them you're going to produce a shape on the glass just by rubbing it with the cloth. The cork will be attracted to the glass as

before, except that this time it'll stick to the glycerine in the outline of whatever shape you've drawn out.

Take the glass and then shine a torch through it and the outline of the image will be projected onto the wall. A white or light-colored wall is good; if you tack up a large piece of white paper, it'll work even better. Your friend won't have a clue how you've managed to produce an image by simply rubbing the "blank" glass.

Fig. 45. *This simple static-electricity trick lets you project any picture onto a nearby wall using a torch.*

26 A TOOTHBRUSH STAND

All you need for this is a fretsaw, a file, some sandpaper, a few pieces of wood—something like holly or sycamore will do the trick—and some glue. The wood needs to be 1/8 in. (3 mm) thick for the top, bottom and sides of the stand and 3/8 in. (9 mm) for the base, which will provide the weight necessary to keep it sturdy. When sized and cut, you'll have seven pieces in total.

The stand itself is 4 1/2 in. (115 mm) high and has four rectangular holes in the top to hold the toothbrushes; as a guide these should be 1/4 x 3/4 in. (7 x 21 mm), but measure your toothbrushes first to make sure they'll fit. Each hole needs to be 1/4 in. (7 mm) in from the side. Cut the top and bottom to measure 2 3/4 x 2 1/4 in. (69 x 57 mm) and the sides so that they're 3 3/4 x 2 in. (95 x 50mm). The base should be 2 3/4 x 2 3/4 in. (69 x 69 mm).

Use the file and sandpaper to round the top of the base neatly. Then take the bottom and cut four mortises into it 1/8 x 1 in. (3 x 25 mm)—each one set 1/8 in. (3 mm) in from the edge. Cut each side so it measures 3 3/4 x 2 in. (95 x 50 mm) and cut a tenon into the bottom of each one. Although you can leave the sides plain, the stand will look more attractive if you use the fretsaw to shape it as shown in the diagram. Finally, you'll need to bevel the edges of each side with a medium file to ensure a neat, tight fit at the sides.

Before you glue anything, fit the sides into the thin base with the mortise-and-tenon joints and check that their chamfers are snug and that the top sits neatly. Make any necessary adjustments and glue the bottom to the base, then refit the sides before gluing the top to all four sides—the mortise-and-tenon joints at the bottom and the bevels at the sides don't need gluing.

Fig.46. *The completed stand. Taking time to ensure all the corners fit snugly will improve both its looks and stability.*

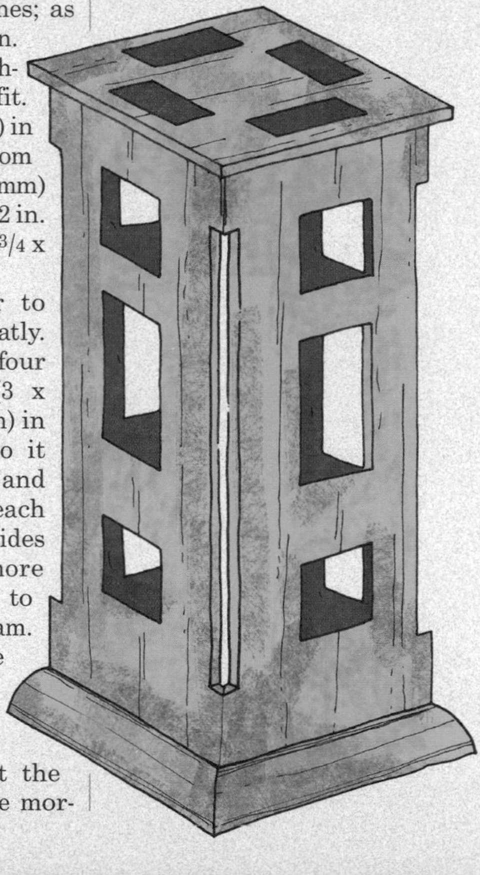

(27) SELF-RUNNING RAILROAD

The idea behind this impressive-looking railway is simple—to let gravity do the work of driving a train—or trains—from one end of the track to the other. When the train arrives, it's raised on a lift, at which point it's ready to begin its journey back to the other end of the track.

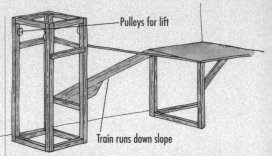

Fig. 47. *A finished tower with one of the slopes and the flat section in the middle.*

The bulk of the model can be made from simple materials like plain battens of wood, the sides of packing cases or cardboard, glue and nails. You'll need some cord and model pulleys for the lifts at either end—and although you can make them, it's probably best to buy the track and trains from a model shop.

Fig. 48 should give you a general idea of what's supposed to happen. The train leaves the tower at one end and travels down the slope, picking up speed before hitting the flat section and slowing down. It then descends again to the bottom of the opposite tower—which is actually a little lift—before being raised to the top. After that it can go back the other way. The idea, of course, is to have two trains running in opposite directions at the same time.

There aren't any detailed measurements for this because the overall size depends on how much space you've got available. It's a good idea, however, to arrange things so that the flat area between the two towers is in a corner so it doesn't take up quite so much space.

Start by making the flat area, as shown in Fig. 47, using packing case wood (or cardboard) and battens for uprights and cross-braces as shown in the diagram. Next get a piece of board about 6 in. (152 mm) wide and rest one end on the edge of the flat area. Tilt the other end up. Find the best angle by running a wheeled toy down it a few times (as a rough guide it should rise 1 ft. (305 mm) every 8 ft. (2438 mm).

When you've worked out the best height for the far end, build the tower as shown in Fig. 47 out of battens screwed into the wall. The tower should be about 18 in. (457 mm) square. Attach the sloping board to a batten screwed across the front of the two and

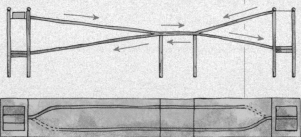

Fig. 48. *Elevation and plan views—arrows indicate the path of the trains.*

make sure it's well secured. Then attach a second board sloping down from the flat area to a cross-batten that's been screwed across the tower at a lower level, for the train to run down.

Repeat this construction at the other end of the flat area to make the second tower. You'll probably need to strengthen each tower with cross-battens at various points, but this will depend largely on the dimensions.

With the towers built, you can add the lifts. Each lift is simply a flat board, notched at each corner so it fits between the uprights; the notches act as guides when the lift goes up and down. Fit the pulleys to the upright battens on the towers as shown in Fig. 47, making sure that the front pair are single pulleys and the back pair are doubles. Drill holes in the lift as shown in Fig. 49 and then thread the cords as shown. You'll need a round cross-bar, with holes drilled at either end to thread the cord through, to act as a handle—when you pull the handle, the lift should rise. When this is working, bring the lift to the top so it's level with the upper track and then nail a crosspiece on the frame to stop the lift going any higher; then do

The Ground Zero Shed

SHED LIFE

If there's one person who took the shed to its outer limits, it's David Hahn. Hahn was a boy scout intent on getting his science merit badge. Driven from the house by his parents (who were unsurprisingly alarmed by the explosions he was routinely setting off in his bedroom) the industrious scout retired to the garden shed. Having made nitroglycerine, aged 14 Hahn decided to make a nuclear reactor. Claiming to be a physics teacher at a local high school, he approached the U.S. Nuclear Regulatory Commission for advice and found them very helpful. He scrounged americium-241 from discarded smoke alarms, thorium-232 from gas lanterns and radium paint from old clocks. By the time his shed was raided, contamination levels were 1000 times greater than normal and no one could go in there without wearing a radiation suit.

the same at the bottom to stop it falling through the floor. After this, build the second lift for the other tower.

Using store-bought track, lay lines along the ramps down to the flat area and back up again. To improve the look of the railroad, fill in the gaps between the tracks with cardboard and paint it. Then clad the towers in the same way.

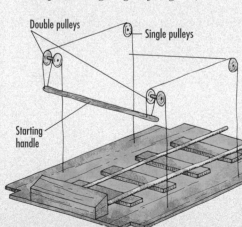

Double pulleys

Single pulleys

Starting handle

*Fig. 49. **The lift mechanism in greater detail—note that the frame supporting the pulleys is not pictured.***

28 A PERFECTLY BALANCED MODEL

This project is an easy way to create an optical illusion. All you need is some plain card, a pair of scissors, and perhaps a bit of Plasticine.

Carefully copy the design of the bird onto some card (if you enlarge it, make sure that the proportions remain the same). Cut it out with a sharp pair of scissors and you'll find you can balance it horizontally by positioning the tip of a pencil at the end of its beak. You can smarten up the bird with crayons (which are better than felt-tips for a job like this) and if the model needs more stability, conceal a pinch of Plasticine beneath the tip of each wing, making sure it's out of sight so as not to spoil the effect.

Although it looks certain that the bird will overbalance and fall on its beak, this is an illusion. The weight behind the point of balance is exactly the same as that in front of it—the spread of the wings and the gap between them fools you into thinking that the bird must topple, when in fact it will appear to hover effortlessly.

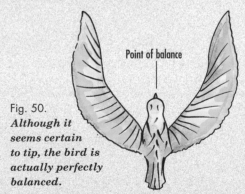

Point of balance

Fig. 50. *Although it seems certain to tip, the bird is actually perfectly balanced.*

29 NATURE'S BOOKMARKS

You can make your own unique bookmarks with some card, glue and a little imagination. If you're the country type, you'll find the decorative raw materials you need on any walk or in your backyard.

Leaves, grasses and pressed flowers can be glued directly onto your bookmark—this should be an oblong of card about 6–8 in. (150–200 mm) long and about 1 1/2 in. (38 mm) wide—and you can make it even snazzier by cutting the bookmark to mimic the shape of whatever you've mounted.

If you can't get out and about, then use pictures cut out of magazines; single images and collages work equally well. A snap of your newborn baby can make a great gift for a grandparent. If you want to cheat a little, a local print shop will laminate your bookmark for a small fee.

Fig. 51. *By using natural materials to decorate your bookmark, you can create a design that is both unique and pleasing to the eye—perfect for an inexpensive but individual present.*

30 A TRADITIONAL BOW

Bow-making takes time, but the results are definitely worth the effort. Finding the right raw material is important—you'll need to use a hardwood sapling that's about 2 in. (51 mm) thick in the middle. You're looking for one that's knot-free and doesn't have any twists.

Cut a length that's as tall as you are and then split it in half down its length so it looks like a "D" shape. Strip off the outer bark. Roughly reduce the width of the wood on the inside surface—called the "belly"—with a sharp knife until it's about 1 in. (25 mm) thick, then spread some glue on the ends.

Take it inside and tie the ends to something long and straight like a bed frame, then slide a couple of wood blocks between the ends of the bow and the bed frame. Then tie the middle of the bow to the frame. The belly of the bow should be facing the frame. Leave for four weeks. At the end, you'll have a sort-of-seasoned piece of wood.

Untie the wood and then with a ruler and pencil draw the shape of the bow as you would see it looking at the belly. Make the handle about 4 in. (101 mm) long and just over 1 in. (25 mm) wide. Start to taper the shape at about 8 in. (203 mm) from each end—taper it down to 1/2 in. (13 mm). Use a coarse file and sandpaper to shape the bow to the outline.

Next you need to put some bend into the bow by removing wood from the belly with a file.

Start at either end of the handle and scrape at right angles to the bow. When you've done a bit, stand the bow on end and test its flexibility. Then remove some more. Pretty soon you'll start to see where the bow is and isn't bending. The idea is that the whole bow should bend evenly apart from the ends and the handle.

When you're happy, make two notches at the sides of either end of the bow, string it with ordinary string so that the ends are pulled back, and leave it overnight. Try it again in the morning—you may need to make further adjustments with sandpaper. Later, if the bow works well, you can use "proper" store-bought bowstring material.

Fig. 52. *Real bow-making takes years to learn. However, you can start right by following the techniques described here—such as binding the bow to a bed.*

(31) STANDARD-LAMP STAND

Good results don't have to involve hard work—both the materials and construction methods used to make this old-fashioned stand are simple.

You'll need four planks of pine: one 5 ft. x 3 in. x 1/2 in. (1.5 m x 76 mm x 13 mm); a second piece measuring 4 ft. x 8 in. x 1/2 in. (1.2 m x 203 mm x 13 mm); another piece which is 3 x 3 x 1 in. (76mm square and 25 mm thick); some batten 4 ft. x 2 in. x 1 in. (1.2 m x 50 mm x 25 mm); and finally 6 ft. of half-round wood, 1/2 in. in diameter (1.8 m and 13 mm).

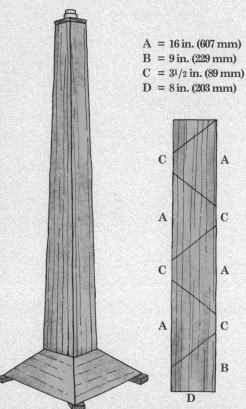

A = 16 in. (607 mm)
B = 9 in. (229 mm)
C = 3 1/2 in. (89 mm)
D = 8 in. (203 mm)

To make the central column, make a mark on the inside face at the same end of each plank that's exactly 2 in. (51 mm) in from the edge. When you glue and nail the planks together, make sure that each one is flush against this mark at one end while the others are fully edge to edge; this produces a column that tapers at the top. Saw off the overlaps at the top and sand to a finish.

Take your top piece and drill a 1/2 in. (13 mm) hole through it. Make sure the top of the stand is level and then glue and nail it on. Cut the batten into two equal halves and then halve each one in the center so you can fit them together like an "X." Screw them to the bottom corners of the stand.

Take the 8 in. (203 mm) piece of wood and mark it up as shown in Fig. 53. This will give you four sides for the bottom of the stand. Mark and cut the wood as accurately as you can to ensure a good fit, then plane and sand it smooth. Test the measurements by leaning the sides against the bottom of the stand and make any necessary adjustments before securing them to the column and the crosspiece with glue and nails. Cover all the joins with lengths of the half-round wood (this will cover a multitude of sins) secured with glue and panel pins. Finally, cut out four small squares from the 8 in. (203 mm) wood and screw them into each corner—the gap at the bottom is for the electrical wire. Finish with fine sandpaper and stain.

Fig. 53. A traditional standard lamp is relatively easy to make and remains something of a design classic—even this basic version looks good.

㉜ PAPER POWERBOATS

This project is ideal if you're looking for ways to have some light-hearted fun in your shed. These simple instructions provide an ingenious way to propel a boat across water.

Start by cutting out a typical rowing-boat shape from ordinary paper. Find the halfway point between the bow and the stern and mark it with a pencil. Use a compass to draw out a small circle, cut a narrow channel from the stern to the circle's edge, then cut out the circle.

Place the boat carefully in a water butt or a bathtub, making sure the surface remains dry, and then add a drop of oil to the center of the circle. As the oil tries to spread across the surface of the water it will be forced down the channel and set up a reaction that will propel the boat across the water.

You can also make a much more sophisticated version that's actually steam-powered. For the "engine" you'll need two hen's eggs. Make a tiny hole in the narrow end of one, suck it dry using a slim straw, then fill it half full with water. Empty the other one and then carefully cut the shell in half with a sharp knife. Next take a large cork lid (from a pickle jar perhaps) and scoop out a half-egg-sized hollow. Glue the half shell into the hollowed cork.

Next you'll need a couple of pieces of wire, which must be supple enough to bend into shape but stiff enough to sup-port the second egg shell with the water in it (when you fit the engine in the boat, these bits of wire can be folded over the sides). Bend them into two frames to support the egg with the hole.

Right, now you need to fill the half shell with cotton wool soaked in some-thing flammable like lighter fluid or methylated spirit. Sit the other egg shell lengthwise on the wire frame. Light the cotton wool, and in a few moments the heat will boil the water in the egg above it. This will force steam out of the hole, which will propel the boat through the water.

Oil goes here

Fig. 54. *When you drop the oil into the center, it's forced down the channel, which pushes the boat forwards.*

Steam

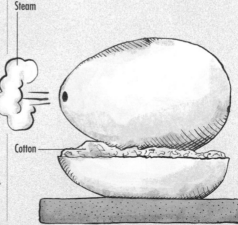

Cotton

CHESSBOARD

For this you'll need a wood such as sycamore, which is good-looking and carries a stain well. Get it planed so that it's 1/4 in. (6 mm) thick and then cut into 12 x 1 3/8 in. (305 x 35 mm) strips. You need eight strips in all. Stain four of them black—or at least dark—using a good-quality stainer to highlight the natural grain of the wood, and leave to dry.

Plane the strips on a shooting board (see page 25) so that they're 1 1/4 in. (32 mm) wide—it's important to make edges as accurate as possible to ensure a good fit. Glue the eight lengths of wood onto a piece of paper, laying the dark and light strips alternately, and all facing the same direction, like lanes in a swimming pool. Glue each strip to its neighbor (as well as to the paper), pushing the edges together as close as you can and wiping away any excess glue. Leave to dry.

Square off one end, plane it true and then mark off a strip 1 1/4 in. (32 mm) wide across the "lanes" so that when you cut it off you'll have a strip made of dark and light squares. Saw it off, plane it true using the shooting board, and then repeat until you've got eight strips of dark and light squares.

Lay them out on a square of 3/4 in. (19 mm) thick plywood so that they form a chessboard. The plywood needs to have a 1 1/2 in. (38 mm) gap all round the edge. You may need to make some fine adjustments to the edges, but when they're all flush you can glue them to the plywood board.

Fill the gap round the outside edge with mitered wood—as if it were a picture frame—and then glue and nail these outside edges in place. You can make the outside edge more decorative if you wish, but plain wood will also serve the purpose.

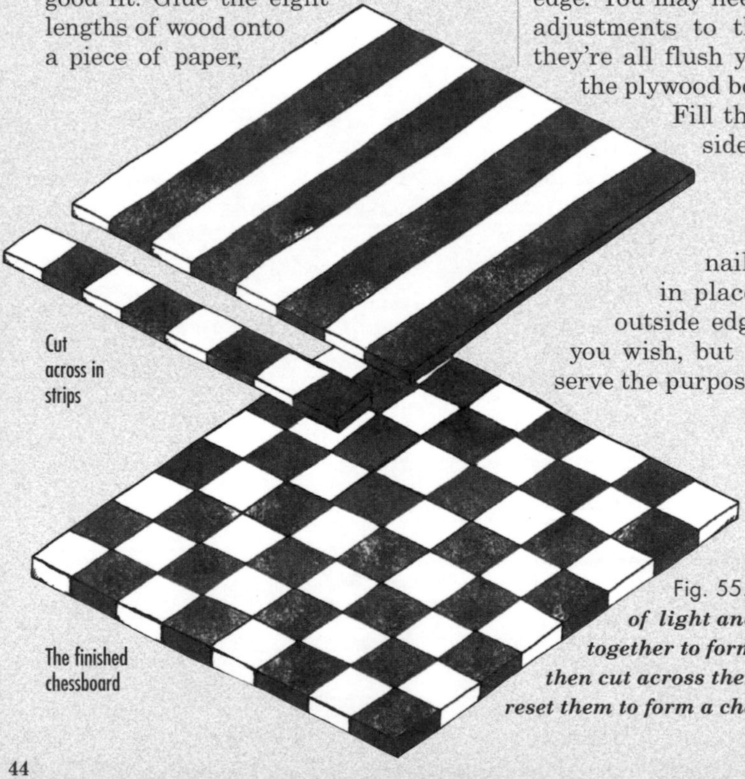

Cut
across in
strips

The finished
chessboard

Fig. 55. *Glue lengths of light and dark wood together to form "lanes" and then cut across them. Finally, reset them to form a chessboard.*

34 THE CURIOUS CROSS

This optical illusion will make people see things that aren't really there. Take a piece of green paper (8½ x 11 in.) and draw or paint a large solid black cross on it. Next, stand the paper up between the leaves of two hardcover books as shown below. Get a piece of 8½ x 11 in. plain white paper (card is even better because there's no show-through) and drop it down in front of the first sheet of paper so that it completely hides the green paper and cross; the edges of the cards should sit between the leaves of the open books on either side.

Get a friend to stare at the green paper and black cross for about 20 seconds. Then drop the white paper down in front of it. Wait a few seconds and then ask your friend if they've noticed anything. Most people will see a red cross on a white background—even though there's nothing actually there. This is because white and red are the two colors that most complement black and green, and so seem to appear when the first piece of paper is hidden.

Position the paper like this

35 THE CANDLE ENGINE

This experiment uses the principle of balance to drive a simple "engine" that is powered by a single candle. To create it, you'll need a couple of glasses, a pair of dishes or saucers (to catch the dripping wax, should you need to keep the table clean) and a couple of pins.

Take the candle and then cut it at an angle at both ends as shown in the diagram so that the wick sticks out. Next, take two pins and stick them into opposite sides of the candle, exactly in the middle; then balance it on the rim of the two glasses. Pop the saucers into place under the candle ends if you need to.

Making sure the candle is properly balanced, light both ends with a match and then wait. After a minute, wax will drip from one end changing the balance of the candle; this end will then rise up because it's lighter. As the other end falls, wax will drip from there and the balance will be restored. The candle "engine" will continue to rock back and forth on its own.

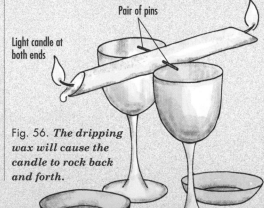

Pair of pins

Light candle at both ends

Fig. 56. *The dripping wax will cause the candle to rock back and forth.*

36 DOG KENNEL

This makes the perfect home for the pooch in your life—especially if you'd prefer that it spend its nights out of doors.

To make the kennel you'll need the following timber: one piece of 96 x 48 x 5/8 in. (2438 x 1219 x 16 mm) exterior grade plywood; one length of 120 x 4 x 2 in. (3048 x 102 x 51 mm); a box of 16d nails; a box of 15/8 in. (41 mm) decking screws; and some paint.

Lay out your wood on a large surface and draw out the various parts of the doghouse as indicated in Figs 57 and 58. Since there're quite a few parts, you may find it useful to label each one in pencil—most will be painted over later (or are inside the kennel) and so won't show. Obviously you want to make the saw cuts as accurate as you can, but don't worry if they're not too precise— you can usually plug the gaps somehow in a simple structure like this, and, anyway, your dog is unlikely to complain.

Take the bottom piece and attach the two sides using the decking screws. The sides go on the outside of the bottom of the kennel, and you should start by securing them at each corner. After that, screw in a couple of extra ones per side. Attach the front and back pieces to the bottom and sides; use one screw at each bottom corner of the front and back pieces and then a further three up each side—this will provide a good solid base for the rest of the kennel.

The roof is clever but remarkably simple to make, and involves screwing on the two roof panels to a central length of wood 24 x 4 x 2 in. (610 x 102 x 51 mm); since the roof is 32 in. (813 mm)

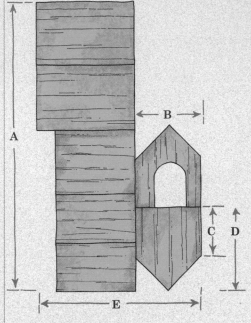

A = 8 ft. (2438 mm)
B = 21 in. (533 mm)
C = 16 in. (406 mm)
D = 27 in. (686 mm)
E = 4 ft. (1219 mm)

Fig. 57. *This is the plan for the main part of the kennel, showing the roof, sides, floor, back and front, complete with dog-sized entrance already cut out.*

long, the smaller roof support—the central length—needs to be positioned in the middle, lengthwise. Then attach the two roof panels using decking screws, as shown in Fig. 58.

The kennel doesn't sit flush to the ground. Instead it's raised on a platform made up of 4 in. (102 mm) high wood. This is important for two reasons. First, because it's off the ground it'll keep the base of the kennel dry, and, second, it helps to keep the cold out, so your dog's

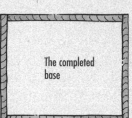

One of the four strips used for
the base of the dog kennel

more likely to enjoy a good
night's sleep. Refer to Fig. 58 to
see how the base goes together.
Note that the right and left sides
are nailed to the inside edges of
the front and back.

The completed base

Fig. 58. *The raised base
(left and above) helps to
insulate the dog kennel
and keep it dry. The
illustration below shows
how the two roof panels
are attached.*

You can now secure the kennel to the base with the decking
screws—screw down from the kennel
into the base, making sure to sink the
screws. Use one screw at each corner
and another two per side.

Finish the whole thing with weatherproof paint and you're done.

Use of decking screws

A few extra points

If you've got a very large—or very
small—dog, you can adjust the sizes
accordingly so long as you keep everything in proportion. Second, if you're
concerned about your dog keeping dry,

buy some asphalt-shingle
sheeting slightly larger than
the overall size of the roof
and fold it round and over, nailing
it into place from underneath—
this will definitely keep the rain
out. Third, whatever you do, measure your dog against the entrance
so it can get in and out.

The Upside-down Shed

In truth, it's not the sheds that are upside
down on Lindisfarne, sometimes called
the Holy Island, off the wild
Northumberland coast in the northeast of
England. Rather, it's the remains of a few
ancient herring boats that have been
pressed into service by the resourceful
locals now that the fishing industry has—
let's not beat about the bush—all but
collapsed. It's a far cry from when these
and hundreds like them made up one of
the largest herring fleets ever to sail from
the east coast of England. Never a
people to let anything go to waste, the
Lindisfarne locals upturned
the few remaining herring
boats and converted them into stor-
age sheds. There they sit—singly and in
rows—for many, one of the first things
they see when they pull into the harbor.
As well as being practical (despite all the
inevitable wear and tear, the boat hulls
are still good at keeping the weather out)
they're rather beautiful—especially the
way the lines on the hull twist and turn,
rather like ribs on the skeleton of a
beached whale, but without the associ-
ated guilt. Or smell.

SHED LIFE

37 LONG-FLYING GLIDER

All you need for this are a couple of sheets of ordinary notepaper, some card, a matchstick and glue. Start by copying the designs for the fuselage, undercarriage, wings, wing struts, tail fin and four wheels. Make enlargements as necessary, but be sure to copy the positions of the slits and dotted lines accurately, because these will help when it comes to making the glider.

You'll notice that there's only one wing, so when you copy this do it on a folded sheet of paper, cut round the pattern through both thicknesses—including the wing-strut slit—and when you've finished, open the paper and you'll have both wings. Next, lightly score along the various dotted lines with the back of a penknife—resting a ruler along the length of the line will keep you accurate.

Start by folding along the outside dotted lines—along the fuselage and in front of the cockpit—and glue the flaps together, remembering to fold and glue the little round front tab inside the nose. Because the paper you're using is light, check carefully all the way along the fuselage before the glue sets to make sure that the shape of the plane is true. Bend the legs of the undercarriage down and glue the flat middle section to the undercarriage. To make the tail fin, glue the fins together and the flaps marked "rudder," then bend the longer sections at right angles and glue the whole thing to the top of the fuselage.

Slip each wing into the slits prepared for it and glue it in place. Fold the strut along the dotted line, glue

it—but don't glue the tabs at each end—and poke it through the slots marked "A" in the fuselage. Push one of the end tabs through the slit in the wing and glue it to the top of the wing; glue the other tab to the underside. Glue the disks together to make two wheels. Use the matchstick for the axle and make sure the wheels are set but that the whole undercarriage moves freely. You'll find that adding a little weight to the nose—perhaps a paper clip—will improve the performance no end.

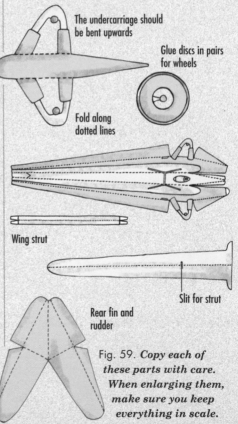

The undercarriage should be bent upwards

Glue discs in pairs for wheels

Fold along dotted lines

Wing strut

Slit for strut

Rear fin and rudder

Fig. 59. *Copy each of these parts with care. When enlarging them, make sure you keep everything in scale.*

38 PAPIER MACHÉ MASK

Papier maché is versatile stuff, and a great way to recycle old newpapers. If you prefer, you can start this fun little project from scratch by making a wire frame, but it's much easier if you can find something that will do as the basis for your mask—like a large plastic milk jug. Exactly how large depends on the size of your head!

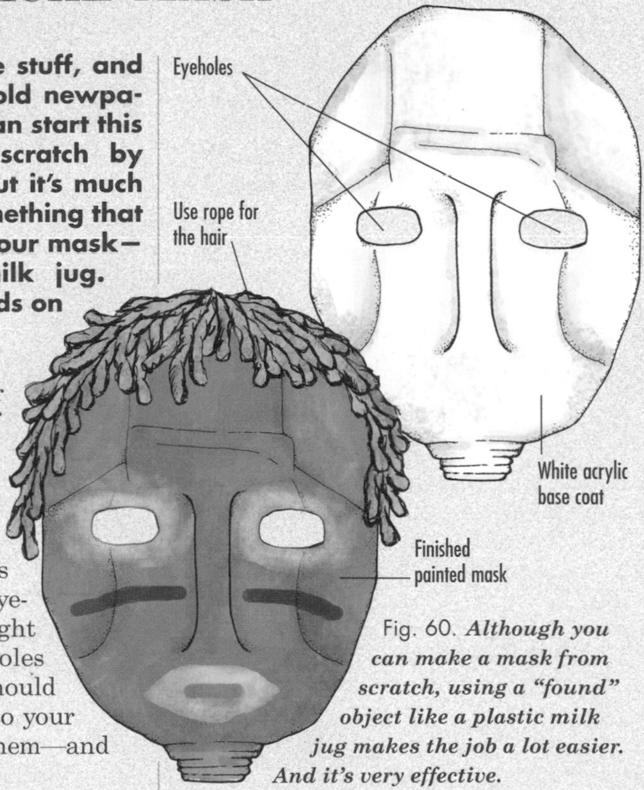

Eyeholes

Use rope for the hair

White acrylic base coat

Finished painted mask

The bit you want to use for the face is the half of the jug with the handle, so cut it in half with a sharp pair of scissors and throw the back away. Wash the inside again and, when it's dry, mark out a pair of eyeholes—you can do this by sight or by making two tiny holes where you think the eyes should go, then holding the mask to your face and looking through them—and then cut them out.

Fig. 60. *Although you can make a mask from scratch, using a "found" object like a plastic milk jug makes the job a lot easier. And it's very effective.*

Get a load of old newspaper and shred it into small easy-to-handle scraps or strips. Pour a couple of cups of hot water into a large bowl, add a couple of cups of white flour and mix until it's lump-free. Coat both sides of the newspaper with the mix—as if you're dipping fish in batter—and then apply to the outside of the mask. Make sure the scraps overlap each other; work in one direction to keep it smooth and squeeze out any air bubbles. When the mask is covered, add another layer, this time working in the opposite direction; then add a third, going back the other way. Then leave the mask to dry, preferably in natural sunlight.

When the mask is completely dry, use acrylic paint to give it a base color—white works best. Wait a couple of hours then add a second coat. Now let the entire mask dry for a whole day.

Paint the face with any design you like—the shape of the jug lends itself to primitive, tribal designs, but it's entirely up to you. Dyed string makes good hair, and can be attached with ordinary glue to the top and sides. Different thicknesses of string work well.

When it's finished , hang the mask on your wall, or staple some elastic to the sides if you want to wear it.

39 CLOCKWORK BOATS

This is a big project and one that will test your woodworking skills and your patience. However, at the end your reward will be a smart clockwork-powered motor boat that will last for years.

For the boat itself you'll need a piece of yellow pine 40 x 8 x 4 1/2 in. (1,016 x 203 x 114 mm); if you can, use an old bit because it's likely to be better seasoned. First, you'll need to plane the block down so that it's 7 x 4 in. (178 x 102 mm); after that, you need to divide the boat into five equal sections. Start by drawing a line lengthwise down the center of the wood, and then dividing it into 6 in. (152 mm) sections using right-angled lines. You'll then have to square the lines on all sides.

Working from the bow of the boat, you should number these lines in your head as 1, 2, 3 and 4 (there's also a line 5, but it's level with the back of the boat). Next, draw on the shape for the hull—as a guide, the width at line 1 should be 4 3/4 in. (121 mm); at line 2 it should be 6 3/8 in. (164 mm) and at line 6 1/4 in. (5,159 mm)—this will give you the curve of the bow

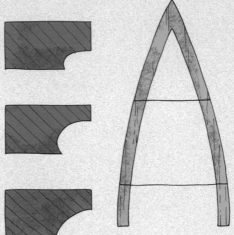

Fig. 62. *The center drawing shows the shape that fits on the front section of the deck.*

Fig. 61. *The three stages of marking up a block of wood to form the hull.*

and stern (see Fig. 61). You can now cut the sides of the block to shape with a saw.

It's not just the width of the boat that varies as you look along those lines, the depth should vary as well. At line 1 it's 4 in. (102 mm), at line 2 it's 3 7/8 in. (99 mm), at 3 it's 3 1/2 in. (89 mm), at 4 it should be 3 in. (76 mm), and at line 5 it's 2 in. (51 mm).

You can't be too hard and fast with these measurements, and you should check the width and depth of each section again when you draw out the curves full size and copy them to section drawings (see Fig. 62). Note that the crossed lines in these sections correspond to the center of the boat and the waterline, so all you need to do is take the width and depth of the boat at the various section points

Fig. 63. *This shows the style of templates you'll need to make the boat's hull.*

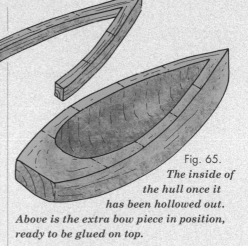

and use that to produce a series of five templates which will help you define the finished shape of the hull (see Fig. 63).

You need to be able to grip the body of the boat upside down while you work on the hull and the best way to do this is with a vice. So that you can hold the boat without damaging the hull, you'll need a clock of wood 18 x 4 x 1 in. (457 x 102 x 25 mm). Drill three 1/4 in. (6 mm) holes to a depth of 21/2 in. (63.5 mm) and then secure it with three 2 in. (51 mm) screws. Don't worry about damaging the boat—you'll be gouging away these bits later on.

Start by cutting the sides to template 3 (see Fig. 63) using a wide sharp chisel and finishing with a spokeshave. Then move toward the position of template 4, and when that's done, go back up the boat to template 2, and then templates 1 and 5. When you've done one side of the

Fig. 64. *Two of the stages you'll have to go through when you shape the hull.*

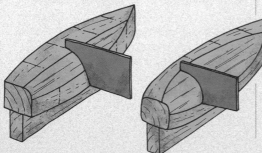

Fig. 65. *The inside of the hull once it has been hollowed out. Above is the extra bow piece in position, ready to be glued on top.*

hull, turn it in the vice and repeat on the other side. When you've done the chiseling and spokeshaving, finish off with coarse sandpaper and then fine glasspaper (Fig. 64).

Take the boat out of the vice and unscrew the holding block. You can now set about removing the interior. Start by boring out a series of holes using a wide center bit. Note that the inside of the hull "hole" starts just beyond line 4 (Fig. 61) and then runs parallel with the sides to the bow; the thickness of the sides needs to be about 1/4 in. (6 mm). If you're not comfortable with shaping the interior of the hull by eye, you can make up a series of four internal templates which you can use to give a smoother, more uniform finish.

With the inside complete, you need to add a bow piece, planed and shaped so it looks like Fig. 65. You can make it from two pieces glued together, but a single piece will be stronger and look more elegant. The wood should be planed to 1 in. (25 mm) deep; the total length is 17 in. (432 mm) and the sides should be about 1/4 in.

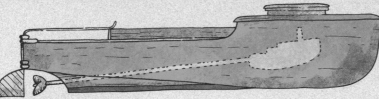

Fig. 68. *The boat with the motor, shaft, propeller and rudder in place.*

(6 mm) thick. Obviously, the outside curve of this piece needs to correspond to the shape of the main hull—you may find it easier to glue it in position first and then finish it off with sandpaper.

Next, you'll need a shop-bought clockwork motor with a propeller and shaft. You'll have to drill a hole for the sloping shaft, as shown in Fig. 68—the motor itself is secured to a small block of wood glued to the inside of the hull. You'll need a keel to add weight and stability to the boat and also to support the propeller properly. Fig. 67 shows the shape of the keel. Your best bet here is to take the boat along to your friendly hardware store or sheet-metal shop and get them to make one up for you. At the same time, get them to make the rudder, which is a piece of sheet brass in a quarter-circle shape 3 x 2 in. (76 x 51 mm). This can be soldered onto a length of 1/8 in. (3.5 mm)

diameter wire, which should be bent at right angles to form the tiller; the actual length of the horizontal part of the tiller —the bit that runs parallel to the deck— should be 6 in. (152 mm). Secure the tiller to the boat with wire staples (Fig. 66).

You should cover the deck with picture backing or some other thin wood—before you glue it into place, work out where the winding key for the motor is and cut a hatch-sized hole there. You can build up a small raised hatchway to cover the hole and also to make the deck more realistic.

When you float the boat you may find it tips to one side and you may have to reposition the motor to compensate. Paint the hull twice and varnish the deck to finish.

Fig. 66. *The rudder, soldered to some wire.*

A = 6 in. (152 mm)
B = 2 in. (59 mm)
C = 3 in. (76 mm)

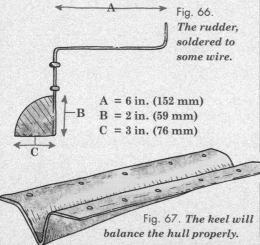

Fig. 67. *The keel will balance the hull properly.*

The Shed Beautiful

Although we're used to beauty contests of all descriptions, the idea of a "shed of the year" sounds pretty bizarre—unless you're Darren Hindley of North Yorkshire. He won Shed of the Year in 2004 for his pub-shed. It's got satellite TV, a stereo, dartboard, barrels for seats and medals on the wall. Visitors, however, are more likely to be found eagerly scanning the photos on the wall, hoping to recognize their own face—having your photo on the wall means free drinks!

SHED LIFE

40 PEPPER'S GHOST

This is based on an old illusion where a "ghost" is reflected onto a stage via a piece of glass. For this miniature version you'll need some card, paints and a sheet of gelatin.

Cut out a piece of white card 10¹/₄ x 2 in. (206 x 51 mm) and draw three lines across it—the first should be 2 in. (51 mm) from the end, the second 5 in. (127 mm) and the third 7 in. (178 mm). Then measure in ¹/₄ in. (6 mm) from the other end and draw a fourth line. Cut the corners of the card at the end as shown to make a tab.

Paint the paper black and let it dry. Then stick it on one end of the gelatin—only about ¹/₈ in. (3 mm) should be stuck to the sheet, leaving the other ¹/₄ in. (6 mm) free. Glue the free end along the top of the section of card with the peephole in it—make sure you stick it to the side with the ghost drawn on it. Score carefully along the four lines you drew across the card and then fold it into a frame. The gelatin sheet should be angled down as shown in the finished drawing below.

Stand near a window so that light shines in through one of the open sides, and look through the hole. You should see the reflection of the ghost projected "floating" in front of the back wall. Make it move by lifting the gelatin sheet up and down.

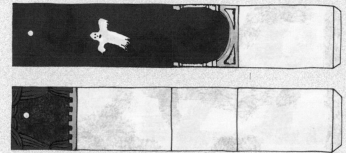

Fig. 69. *Copy the top design onto the inside of your card and the design underneath it on the other side.*

Fig. 70. *The complete illusion in miniature—move the gelatin sheet up and down and the ghost will "float."*

On one side of the card draw or paint a stage with curtains and, when it's dry, make a viewing hole in the middle near the top. On the other side draw the ghost, add an arch and then, using the blackest ink you can find, paint the areas with the hole, the ghost, the arch and the tab a solid black.

Get a 2 x 3 in. (51 x 76 mm) sheet of stiff gelatin and a strip of 2 x ³/₈ in. (51 x 10 mm) paper.

41 SUNDIAL

This sundial will help you to keep a track of time as you while away the hours in your garden. To make it you'll need a pin, ruler, protractor, some card about 10 in. (254 mm) long and a little wider than the protractor, and a plastic drinking straw.

Start by drawing three lines across the card with the ruler. For this sundial we're assuming you live at a latitude of 50 degrees or more. The lines should be drawn across the card at 6/16 in. (10 mm), 315/16 in. (100 mm) and 51/2 in. (140 mm); think of these lines as being labeled 1,2 and 3. Mark a point at the center of the first line (point A) and another at the center of the third line (point B). Draw a single line connecting the two points.

Next, put the center of your protractor on point A and draw round it. Make a hole through point A

Points north   Mark other side the same

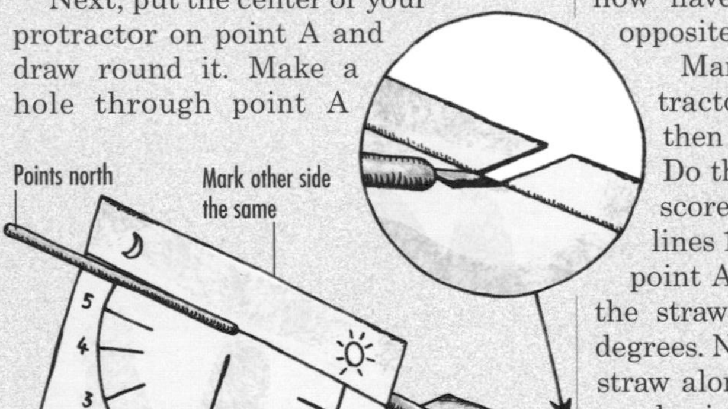

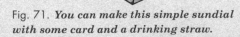

Fig. 71. *You can make this simple sundial with some card and a drinking straw.*

with a pin, flip the card and, putting the center of the protractor over the pinhole, draw round it again. You should now have two semicircle shapes on opposite sides of the card.

Mark out intervals round the protractor shape at 15 degrees and then number the hours as shown. Do the same for both sides. Gently score and then fold the card along lines 1, 2 and 3. Make the pinhole at point A a bit bigger so you can push the straw through at an angle of 90 degrees. Next, move the other end of the straw along the line that joins point A and point B until the angle is the same as the latitude of where you live (for example, London is 51.5 degrees). When you've found the correct position, fold up a tab of card to hold the straw in place.

The straw is what's called the "gnomon." The shadow it casts will fall on the hour lines on the top side of the dial during summer, and on the underside in winter.

42 HOW TO MAKE A MAP

Making a map is easier than you think, and by starting small with this example you'll understand some important principles which will help you should you decide to try something more complex.

Start by tying three sticks together as shown in Fig. 72, so they make an "A" shape. Ensure that that distance between the two "feet" is 3 ft. (915 mm). Now you've got your measuring stick, you need to choose a triangle of land to map. This can, of course, be anywhere you like, but it helps if it's not too big, if there are three good landmarks—one at each corner—and that you can walk to any landmark and see the other two.

Put one point of the measuring stick at one of the corners and then turn it 180 degrees around the other point in the direction of the second corner. "Walk" the stick between the first two corners like this, keeping count of the number of turns. Repeat for the other two sides and then draw the triangle to scale.

Next, walk along one side of the triangle, all the time looking at the landmark on the third corner. When anything comes between you and the landmark, use the measuring stick to pace off the distance and make a note of it. When you've recorded everything you can see by walking that side of the triangle, walk up the second side and repeat the exercise. By combining the measurements you've taken from the two sides you'll be able to put together a useful little map.

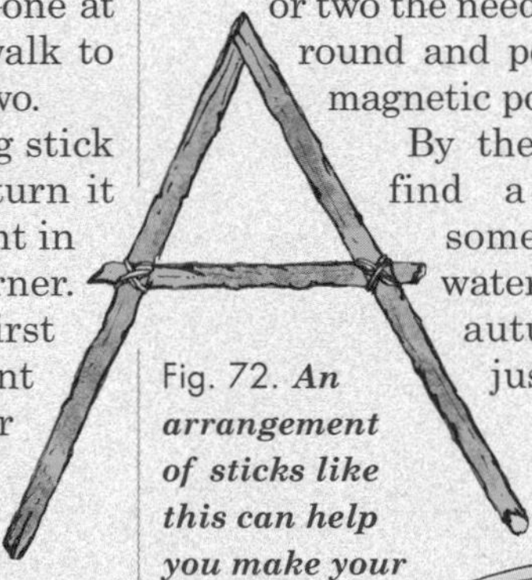

Fig. 72. *An arrangement of sticks like this can help you make your own map.*

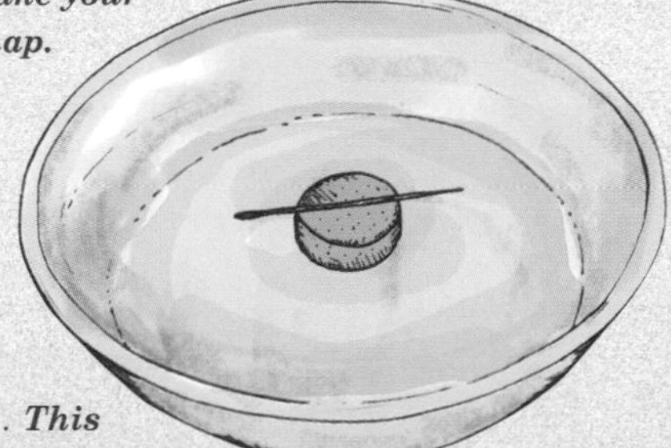

43 COMPASS

Making a compass is simple. All you need is a sewing needle, a magnet—even a fridge magnet will probably do—a bit of cork, some clear tape and a bowl to hold some water.

Take the needle and then run the magnet over it 20 times from the eye to the point to magnetize it. Then get a cork from an old bottle and cut a thin 1/8 in. (3 mm) slice off—as if you were slicing a sausage. Tape the needle to one side of the cork so that both ends of the needle stick out (be careful not to prick yourself). Put the bowl of water on a flat surface and then gently lay the cork-and-needle onto the surface. After a moment or two the needle will swing slowly round and point to the nearest magnetic pole.

By the way, if you can't find a piece of cork, something light but water-resistant (like an autumn leaf) will do just as well.

Fig. 73. *This simple compass will reliably point to magnetic north.*

44 PIPE RACK

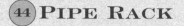

Pipes are different. First, you don't throw them away when you've finished smoking; second, you need somewhere to store them. So give your pipes the setting they deserve with this satin walnut pipe rack. (I've used walnut, but you could use a bit of old reclaimed mahogany.)

You'll need four pieces of wood: a 10 x 6$1/2$ x $1/4$ in. (250 x 165 x 6 mm) back; an upper shelf of 7 x 1 x $3/16$ in. (178 x 25 x 5 mm); a lower shelf of 8 x 1$3/4$ x $3/16$ in. (203 x 44 x 5 mm); and bottom shelf supports which are 2$3/4$ x $3/4$ x $3/16$ in. (69 x 19 x 5 mm).

Once you've cut out the back, mark it out carefully into 1 in. (25 mm) squares and then draw the design directly onto the wood. Mark the positions of the two shelves and the bottom shelf supports in dots, using a ruler and a pin. The underside of the lower shelf is 1 in. (25 mm) from the bottom, and the lower side of the upper shelf is 2$1/2$ in. (63 mm) from the top. Both shelves are centered on the back and the supports are placed $1/2$ in. (12.5 mm) in from the edge. Cut out the shape using a fretsaw and tidy it up with sandpaper. Cutting out the two

square holes will enhance the look. Drill a hole at the top to hang the rack.

Gently round the front edges of both shelves with sandpaper. Then drill four $5/8$ in. (16 mm) holes in the top shelf. To position them, mark the halfway point on each side of the shelf—this will be $1/2$ in. (12.5 mm) from the edge—and draw a light pencil line, running through the center of each hole. Measure in $7/8$ in. (22 mm) and mark it with a pinprick. That's the center of your first hole. Measure 1$3/4$ in. (44 mm) along from that point and make another mark for the center of the second hole. Continue until all four holes are marked, then drill them out.

To make the shelf supports, place the last piece of wood horizontally on your bench and mark a point $1/4$ in. (6 mm) in from each end on the bottom. Mark the halfway point along the top edge; measure down $3/16$ in. (5 mm) and make another point. Draw a curve that joins the three points and then saw it out. Saw the wood in half to make the supports and glue them in place. Finally, glue on the two shelves, adding a $1/2$ in. (12.5 mm) screw to each from the back.

A = 6$1/2$ in. (165 mm)
B = 10 in. (250 mm)
C = 1$3/4$ in. (44 mm)
D = 1 in. (25 mm)
E = 7 in. (178 mm)
F = 1$3/4$ in. (44 mm)
G = 8 in. (203 mm)

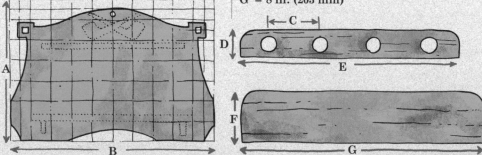

45 PAPER BALLS AND TOPS

Here's an excellent running wheel you can make from a piece of card—chasing this in high winds will help to build up the speed and lung capacity you'll need for the second part of the project . . .

Take a sheet of thin cardboard and draw a circle of 3 in. (76 mm) in diameter. Then draw another circle inside with a diameter of 1³/₄ in. (44 mm). Next divide the inner circle into quarters by drawing two more diameters at right angles to each other. Find the halfway point between one of these quarters and draw another diameter across the inner circle. Keep going until it's divided into 16 segments.

You need to cut all of the long sides of these triangles with a sharp pen or craft knife and then turn the triangles up and then down in turn as shown in Fig. 74. On a windy day you'll have your work cut out keeping up with this one as it tears down the street!

Got your fitness levels up? Then you're ready for the next challenge. Draw a circle 2 in. (51 mm) in diameter on a piece of card and then cut it out. Draw six rectangles on the card with a pencil and then, with a sharp knife, cut along the inner long edge and both sides. Then fold up all the rectangles in the same direction.

Next, take a drawing pin (or one that's slightly longer, if you can find it) and push it up through the center of the circle so that the pin protrudes on the same side as the open flaps. Get a cotton reel and hold it over the circle so that the hole in the end of the reel is over the point of the pin and as close as you can get it to the circle without touching any of the flaps. Blow like crazy and the top will begin to spin—if you've got enough puff, it can get up to a good speed.

What's happening is that the shape of the top creates a vacuum between it and the cotton reel, so that the air underneath supports the top and allows it to spin freely—as long as you keep blowing.

The harder version, with six rectangles

Fig. 74. *This is the one you need your puff for—so long as you can keep blowing, the top will spin and rise into the air!*

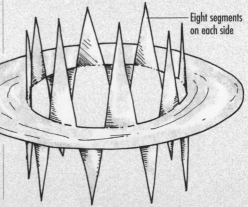

Eight segments on each side

46 THE CHAIR LADDER

It's a chair! It's a ladder! Steady, there—actually, it's both.

For this you'll need the following wood, planed and squared: 13 ft. 6 x 1¹/2 x 1¹/2 in. (4,110 x 38 x 38 mm) pine; 9 ft. x 1¹/2 x ¹/2 in. (2,740 x 38 x 13 mm) of batten; 16 ft. 6 x 3 x ³/4 in. (5,030 x 76 x 19 mm) of pine; 7 ft. 6 x 3 x ¹/2 in. (2,280 x 76 x 13 mm) of pine.

Make the back frame from the 1¹/2 in. (38 mm) square pine. Cut two 3 ft. (914 mm) uprights and halve them at the top. Cut a piece 18 in. (457 mm) long from the same wood and halve it at both ends, and then screw it carefully across the uprights at the top.

Next, cut two pieces, 18 in. (457 mm) long from the 1¹/2 x ¹/2 in. (38 x 13 mm) batten and screw them across the uprights—the top of the first should be 9 in. (228 mm) from the bottom, the top of the second 17 in (431 mm). This back frame is shown in Fig. 75.

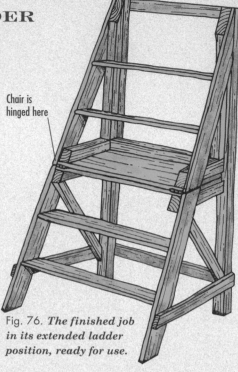

Chair is hinged here

*Fig. 76. **The finished job in its extended ladder position, ready for use.***

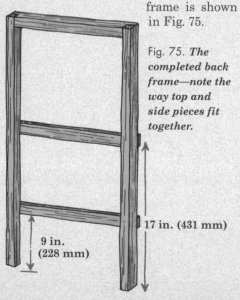

*Fig. 75. **The completed back frame—note the way top and side pieces fit together.***

17 in. (431 mm)

9 in. (228 mm)

Now it's time to make the seat stays and front legs. Cut two lengths of 17 in. (431 mm) for the legs, and two of 18 in. (457 mm) of the 1¹/2 in. (38 mm) square pine for the stays. Halve one end of both 17 in. (431 mm) pieces, 1¹/2 in. (38 mm) from the end; halve both ends of the 18 in. (457 mm) pieces on the same side of the wood. Screw two pieces of each length together at right angles to form two "L" shapes (Fig. 77).

Screw on a crosspiece of 3 x ³/4 in. (76 x 19 mm) at right angles to the seat stay, so that its furthest edge is 8¹/4 in. (209.5 mm) away from the front corner. Saw off the overlapping corners flush to the stay and leg, and then saw the bottom of both legs to the same angle as the inside edge of the crosspiece. Repeat for the other side (Fig. 76).

Screw the seat stays to the back-frame uprights, level with the top of the middle batten. Next, cut two more crosspieces of 3 x 3/4 in. (76 x 19 mm) wood and screw them into the seat stays next to the other two. Cut any overlap at the top and angle them at the bottom so they sit flush to the floor.

Cut two lengths of 1 1/2 x 1/2 in. (38 x 13 mm) to fit from the outside of the back frame, level with the bottom batten, to the front edge of the crosspiece you've just fitted. Measure off two more pieces, to fit from the inside back corner of the piece you've just fitted to the inside top of the crosspiece nearest the back of the chair and, screw them in.

You've still got a gap at the front of the chair, so measure the distance between the two front legs and cut a piece of 1 1/2 in. (38 mm) square wood to fit. Use three 3 in. (76 mm) screws at each end, right through the leg, the stay and the new front piece.

Having spent the day building what looks like a chair with no actual seat, you're now going to go one better—cut it in half. You need to make the cut through the two horizontal stays, making sure that it's at the same angle as the two pairs of crosspieces. Most important, the cut needs to go through the stays without damaging either of the crosspieces.

Separate the two parts and, using 3 x 1/2 in. (76 x 13 mm) wood, attach boards to make a seat; by separating them like this, you'll ensure that you don't accidentally board over where you just made the cut. Screw a pair of 1 1/2 in. (38 mm) square hinges where the front and back parts join so that the front can fold over against the back of the frame.

With the front folded over (to make the ladder shape) you can mark off the steps. The bottom of the first step should be 6 in. (152 mm) from the floor, the second is 13 in. (330 mm) up, the seat makes the third step, and the fourth is 6 in. (152 mm) up from that; the final step is 12 1/2 in. (317 mm) from the top of the seat. You can secure the steps at either end with two screws, but for a longer-lasting chair ladder, let them into the sides by about 1/4 in. (6 mm).

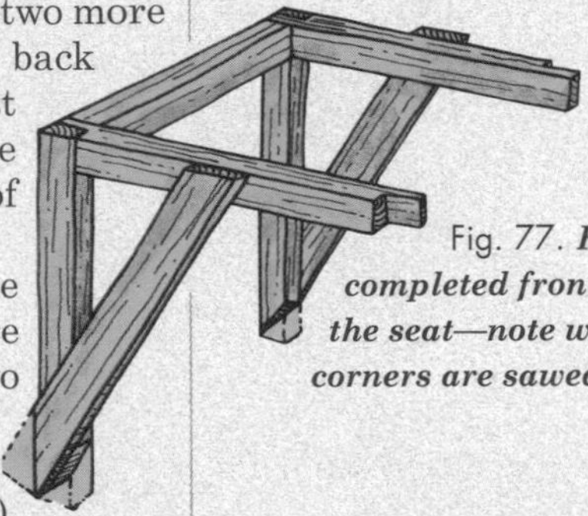

Fig. 77. *Here's the completed front portion of the seat—note where the corners are sawed off.*

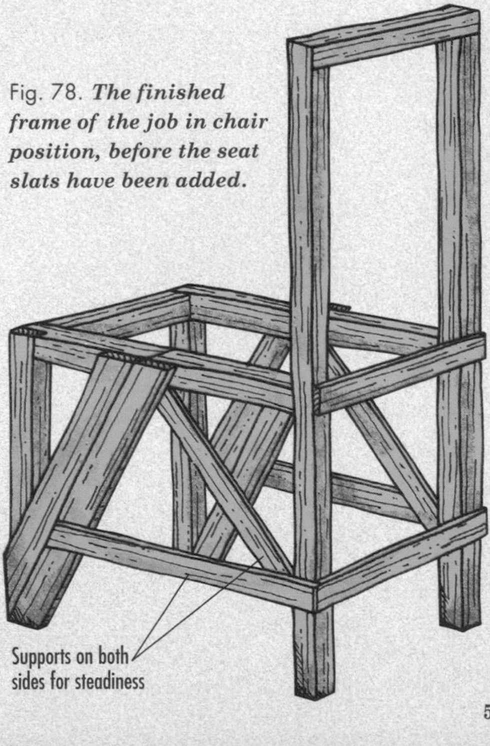

Fig. 78. *The finished frame of the job in chair position, before the seat slats have been added.*

Supports on both sides for steadiness

47 SPRING-TRAP CAR

For this project you'll need a mouse-trap and two 3/16 in. (4 mm) metal rods. These need to be about 9/16 in. (15 mm) longer than the mousetrap is wide, so their precise length depends on the size of the trap. You'll also need four eyehole screws (with eyes large enough for the rods to go through), some plywood for the wheels, some small washers with a 3/16 in. (4 mm) inside diameter, two rubber bands and some string.

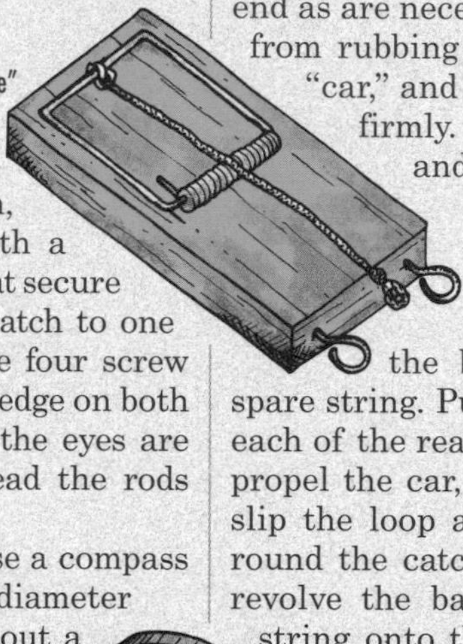

The finished "engine"

Remove the wire catch that keeps the trap open, the cheese holder and, with a pair of pliers, the staples that secure them to the trap. Put the catch to one side. Carefully screw in the four screw eyes 5/16 in. (8 mm) from the edge on both of the short sides, so that the eyes are lined up and you can thread the rods through to act as axles.

Get your plywood and use a compass to draw four circles with a diameter of 2 15/16 in. (75 mm). Bore out a 3/16 in. (3.7 mm) hole in the middle of each circle—this should let you feed through the axles but will also give a nice, tight fit. Cut out the wheels and files and sand them flat.

Cut the rods so that they're the width of the trap plus twice the thickness of the plywood wheels plus 4/16 in. (5 mm), then file the ends with a small bevel.

Use a hacksaw to cut a small notch in one of the axles about a third of the way along and then widen the slot with a file. Cut off a 5/16 in. (7 mm) piece of the catch you removed earlier and then glue the wire into the slot you just cut; the wire should stick out from the axle on one side, with the other side flush. Leave the glue to dry completely.

Find the back of the "car" (where the jaws are when the trap is set) and thread the axle with the wire catch on it through the screw eyes (you'll have to remove one of them and then screw it back in). Add as many washers at either end as are necessary to keep the wheels from rubbing against the side of the "car," and then push the wheels on firmly. Then add the front axle and wheels.

Tie your string to the jaws of the trap and then tie a small loop at the other end, level with the back axle. Cut off any spare string. Put an elastic band round each of the rear wheels for traction. To propel the car, open the jaws by hand, slip the loop at the end of the string round the catch on the rear axle, and revolve the back wheels to wind the string onto the back axle. When the trap's completely open, release the car and it will run across the floor.

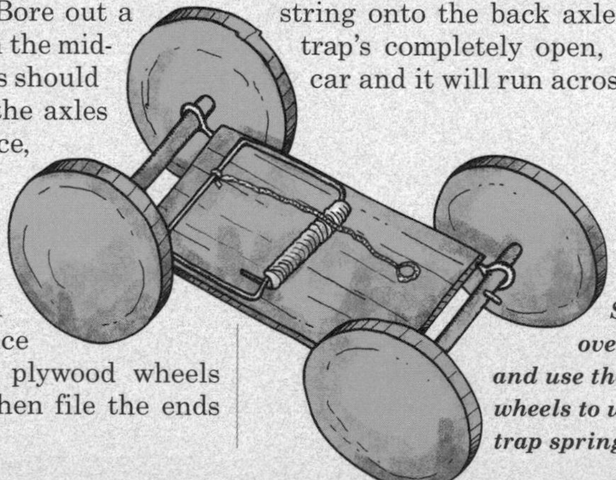

Fig. 79.
Slip the ring over the pin, and use the back wheels to wind the trap spring open.

48 BOOMERANG

This remarkable throwing weapon is world-famous for its ability to return to its owner, and, although the real thing is both dangerous and demanding, you can have a lot of fun designing toy boomerangs of different shapes and sizes out of ordinary cardboard.

The first one—shown below—is the classic Australian boomerang. It is the easiest to make, so try that first and then see how you get on with the others. Make the model about 3 in. (76 mm) across and use thin, but stiff card—a plain postcard will do. Make the outlines as even as you can.

To throw it, take an ordinary-sized paperback book and lay the boomerang of your choice flat on it with the curve facing away from you. Then take a pencil in your other hand and flick the boomerang forward. You'll find the results quite effective.

For the third model, place two of the "spokes" on the book and flick the third; for the fourth have the first bend facing toward you resting on the book and flick the other one; for the last one, the long bit goes on the book and you flick the shorter handle. Great fun.

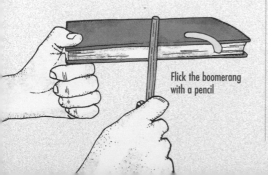

Flick the boomerang with a pencil

49 WOODEN MALLET

This is a handy tool with a range of uses—and it's easy to make.

You'll need hardwood to make a handle 10¹/₂ x 1 x ³/₄ in. (267 x 25 x 19 mm); two short sections for the head measuring 2¹/₄ x 1¹/₄ x ³/₄ in. (57 x 32 x 19 mm); and two long head sections of 3¹/₂ x 2¹/₄ x ³/₄ in. (89 x 57 x 19 mm).

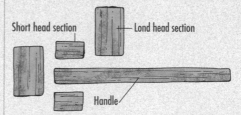

Short head section — Lond head section

Handle

First, glue the short sections to the top of the handle as shown below and let the glue dry. Then glue the larger sections on either side of the head—so you make a sort of sandwich—and let them dry. If you've got a clamp, use it to hold the sections together; if not, improvize by laying the hammer flat on a desk, covering the top with a few sheets of old newspaper and laying something heavy on the top.

Once the glue's set, drill a ³/₈ in. (10 mm) hole through the side of the head, paint some glue onto the sides of the hole and then hammer in a dowel. When that's dry, finish off with sandpaper to smooth the handle and the head of the hammer.

50 COLLAPSIBLE MUSIC STAND

This useful stand—designed for the budding musician—can also be used for holding a newspaper or as a paper holder in an office.

First, you'll need a heavy base—otherwise your stand won't stand up properly. Any sturdy block of wood will do, but you'll need to spend some time rounding the edges with a chisel and using sandpaper to make it look more attractive. Alternatively, a large food container about three-quarters full with sand and sealed with tape will do the trick. You'll also need three dowel rods, 3/8 in. (10 mm) in diameter and 15 in. (380 mm) long, as well as some elastic and some little wooden pegs from a craft or hobby shop.

Drill a hole into the wood base (or container lid) to take the vertical dowel, and make sure it's a good, tight fit. If you're using a metal container, fold some elastic tape around the hole so that the sharp edges don't damage the dowel rod. Take two of the dowel rods and drill six equidistant holes to hold the ends of the elastic; these can be secured with the wooden pegs either by jamming or gluing them in place. The elastic itself should be cut into 8 in.(200 mm) lengths before you attach each one. Next, tap a small peg into the top of the vertical dowel rod so that it fits into a hole drilled into the crosspiece.

Get a bulldog clip about 1 1/2 in. (38 mm) long and prise out one of the side plates. Make a couple of holes at each end of the plate and secure it to the crosspiece with two small nails, then reassemble the clip.

Finally, you'll need to make a small hole through the vertical dowel rod to hold the lower crosspiece. Thread some sturdy—but bendable—wire through the hole and then twist it into the shape shown in the diagram.

Fig. 80. *The finished stand, ready for the musician—the spring clip holds the music securely in place.*

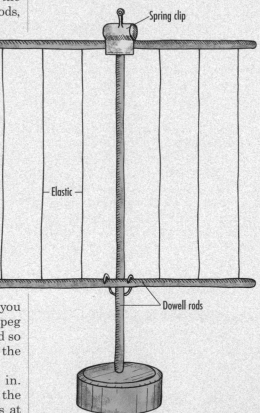

Spring clip

Elastic

Dowell rods

51 BOXING BILL

Fancy a fight? This little guy always does. To make him, you'll need a sheet of three-ply plywood, a fretsaw and some sandpaper. Copy the drawings on this page as exactly as you can. You can obviously increase or decrease the overall size of your fighter so long as you keep everything in proportion.

It's really worth spending a bit of time at the start getting the shape and the dimensions as close to these originals as possible—if you do, your fighter will look more realistic. Cut out all the parts with a fretsaw and then round the edges with sandpaper, particularly his arms and legs; you can also make these as muscly as you like. Note that the front and side views of the fighter are only for reference and that his entire body must be made from a single piece of wood. Note too that the lower part of the body has two flat "hips" which prevent the legs from moving up too high and looking unnatural.

Make a hole in each leg and then through the body. Then attach the limbs using a brass-wire rivet. Make sure the body moves naturally on the legs and then fit them into the slots on the base; secure them with a little wood glue.

Make a hole in the right arm and then screw it into the body, leaving the arm loose enough to move freely. Next, pop a small pin into the back edge of the right arm, almost at the top, and tie a length of cotton to it. Attach a tiny screw eye to the back of the right leg at the hip and another at the ankle, and thread the cotton through them. Wire rivet the two pieces of the left arm together at the elbow, then attach the upper arm to the body with a screw—put a washer between the arm and the body. Fix a pin and two small screw eyes to the back of the arm and the left side of the body respectively (as you did for the right arm) and then thread through some cotton.

Finally, connect the forearms to the body using pieces of wire with an eye at each end – these revolve around small screws attached to the forearms and the body as shown in the diagram. Attach some strong elastic to the back of the right leg and the back of the body. Pull the cotton threads one at a time and Bill will start to fight.

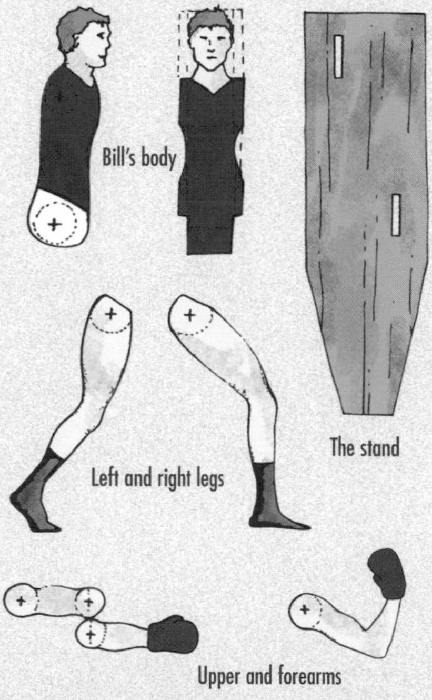

Fig. 81. ***The parts that make up Bill's body. Aim to make them twice the size, keeping everything in proportion—and note where parts go so that he moves correctly.***

52 SIMPLE ELECTRIC MOTOR

Take some paper clips, drawing pins, some enamel-insulated wire, a block of wood, a battery and some small, round-nose pliers. Put them together and at the end you'll have a working electric motor.

Fig. 82 shows the completed motor. The horizontal piece in the middle, called the armature, is what will spin around, powered by the battery—if all goes well, it should spin at a fair old lick.

For the base, you'll need a piece of wood 4 x 4 x 1/2 in. (102 x 102 x 13 mm). If you want to improve the finish of this with a coat of varnish, then do it before you start making the motor.

The first things to make are the two field coils. Using the pliers, open a paper clip and create a loop at each end by wrapping it round something like a large nail; then make a half loop in the middle so you can secure it to the base with a drawing pin. You can see the finished shape in Fig. 84. Next, take some 26 SWG enameled copper wire and wind 50 turns of it onto each arm of the coil. Each turn needs to be tight against the previous one, and you must make sure that they're wound in opposite directions. Remember to make sure that there's enough wire left at each end to make the necessary connections.

Make the armature by bending a second paper clip into a sort of cross (Fig. 83) and winding the parts that are doubled with 25 continuous turns of enameled wire in the same direction. Spend some time getting the paper clip as symmetrical as possible and ensure that the coils are as identical as you can make them; the closer you get to symmetry here the smoother your armature will run. Again, you'll need to leave enough

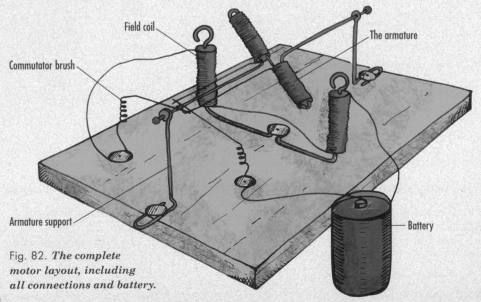

Field coil

Commutator brush

The armature

Armature support

Battery

Fig. 82. *The complete motor layout, including all connections and battery.*

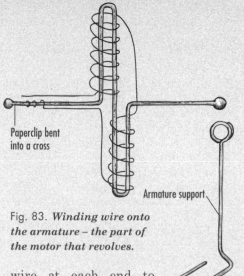

Paperclip bent into a cross

Armature support

Fig. 83. *Winding wire onto the armature – the part of the motor that revolves.*

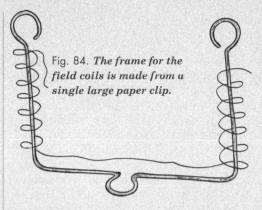

Fig. 84. *The frame for the field coils is made from a single large paper clip.*

wire at each end to make your connections. Scrape each end clean and wind one tightly round one end of the armature, bending the other one straight so it runs parallel. These form what's called the commutator.

Take two more paper clips and bend them into the second shape shown in Fig. 83. These will support the armature, and the eyes at the top must be bent so that it can revolve freely. Another consideration is that each eye should stand at the same height above the board in order to keep the armature level—otherwise it won't rotate freely.

Next, get two short lengths of the enameled wire and scrape the ends clean. Then coil the middle sections of each piece to form a spring shape. These wires are designed to brush lightly against the commutator as it—and the entire armature—spins around.

You're now ready to assemble the motor. Start by securing the field coils to the center of the base with a drawing pin. Then put the armature supports in place, again using a drawing pin for each. Slip the armature through the two loops and give it a twirl. You're looking to make the wired part of the armature revolve exactly in the middle, between the two field coils. The narrower the gap between the armature and the coils, the faster your motor will turn. A bit of Plasticine at either end of the armature spindle will keep it from falling out; when you're satisfied that everything's correctly positioned you can replace this with a drop of solder.

Fix the two commutator brushes to the main board with drawing pins and then you're ready to wire up the whole thing. Find the two free ends of wire coming off the field coils, attach one to a battery and secure the other under the drawing pin holding one of the brushes. Then connect the free end of the second brush to the other end of battery. Check again to make sure that the brushes are correctly positioned against the commutator and turn the armature once gently with your fingers. It should start to spin straight away. If it doesn't, try switching around the wires to the battery and make sure that the brushes are actually touching the commutator. Finally, check and clean any wire ends that you had to scrape. That should solve the problem.

53 BAS-RELIEF PHOTOGRAPH

This is a raised photo that produces a marvelous old-fashioned effect, similar to that of a head on a coin. You'll need a standard-sized portrait photo of yourself—or your subject— in profile. Take the print and immerse it in formalin (this is a mixture of formaldehyde and water that you can buy from a pharmacist) for about ten minutes so it hardens. Then wash it under the tap and leave it to dry.

Make a frame press from stiff cardboard. You'll need two frames, both of which should sit neatly round the photo, leaving the picture in the center, but of a size that they can be clamped around it.

Next, mix one part of white starch to three parts of cold water and make a paste. Add six parts of boiling water and stir over the heat for about five minutes. Let it cool and then squeeze out any lumps with a piece of muslin cloth. Put some tracing paper over the photo and trace the outline of the head, then transfer the outline to a thin piece of cardboard (the same size as the photo) by rubbing over it with a pencil. Take care that the outline on the cardboard is in exactly the same position as the head on the photo by comparing the two, then use a sharp knife to cut the outline out of the cardboard.

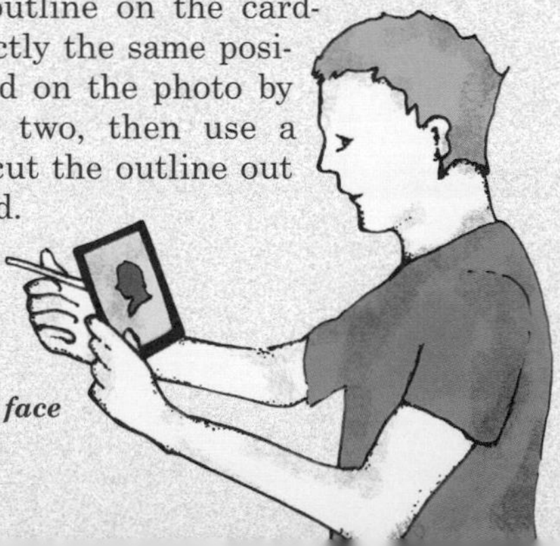

Fig. 85. *Hold the frame in front of you and work the face towards you.*

Apply the starch paste evenly to the back of the photo and then take a piece of thick blotting paper and make a blotting-paper-paste photo "sandwich." Put this under a heavy book for 15 minutes to soften the photo. Line up the cardboard cut-out over the photo and put the lot between the two frames—secure them top and bottom with heavy bulldog clips. Hold the frame with one hand and then use a moulding tool—a toothbrush handle will do—to work the face of the photo toward you, applying slightly more pressure to the nose, cheeks and skull. You must do this carefully or the photo will split. Afterward, pushing the eye and the nostril gently back in from the front will improve the realism of the result.

Leave until completely dry and then mount the photo on some card, supporting the raised part of the photo with a little cotton wool.

Fig. 86. *Use bulldog clips on the top and bottom to secure the cardboard frames.*

54 ADJUSTABLE STILTS

See the world from a different perspective with this pair of adjustable stilts. You'll need two pieces of planed pine 6 ft. (1.83 m) long and 1 1/2 in. (38 mm) square for the stilts and another two pieces that are 5 x 3 x 1 1/2 in. (127 x 76 x 38 mm) for the footrests.

Measure 4 ft. (1.2 m) from the end of each stilt and then plane off the corners. This will make it easier to hold the stilts. Finish off the edges with sandpaper.

Next, round the bottom 6 in. (152 mm) of each stilt as shown in the drawing—this will prevent the corners from wearing down and the wood from splitting. When you've done both stilts, lay them along a bench side by side and, using a square, draw a pencil line across both of them 9 in. (228 mm) up from the bottom. Measure a further 3 in. (76 mm) up from the first mark and draw another line, then carry on marking lines in the same way until you're 2 ft. (600 mm) up from the bottom.

Measure in 1/4 in. (6 mm) from the edge on one of the lines and mark it. Then use a 3/8 in. (10 mm) drill bit to bore through the wood—as the drill comes out the other side, flip the wood and finish the hole from that side. Do the same for every pencil line and then cut out the wood between the holes and the edge of the stilts. Make the footrests by sawing off the corners of the smaller pieces of wood—from 2 ft. (50 mm) down the long side to halfway down the short one. Sand everything down.

Get a local sheet-metal shop to knock up four iron plates 4 1/2 x 1 1/2 x 3/16 in. (114 x 38 x 5 mm). Get each one fitted with a 2 x 3/8 in. (50 x 10 mm) long bolt with two washers and a wing nut. They'll also need to countersink the two screw holes as shown in the diagram. Fix the plates to the front and back of the stilts with 1 1/2 in. (38 mm) wood screws, making sure you reverse one plate from each pair so the screw points don't meet in the middle of the stilts. Each plate must be positioned 1/2 in. (12.5 mm) from the top of the block, and the center of the wing nut hole must be exactly 1 1/4 in. (31 mm) from the longest side of the block.

Fit the footrests as shown in the diagram, then thread and tighten the wing nuts by hand.

Fig. 87. *The finished stilt with the footrest bolted into position in one of the grooves. You'll need two stilts.*

One of the footrests

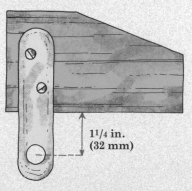

1 1/4 in. (32 mm)

55 THE PACKING-CASE BOOKCASE

The trick to making a good bookcase from wooden packing cases is to find the best materials you can and then do everything possible to conceal their origin—otherwise it's just going to look like a stack of packing cases.

You'll need four packing cases, all the same size—unsurprisingly—that you can stack on top of each other. Nail two supports to the bottom case to form a stand—these should be about 1 in. (25 mm) wide and between 2 in. (50 mm) and 3 in. (75 mm) high.

The next step is to camouflage those cases. Make a plinth from wood about

1 in. (25 mm) thick and high enough so it's level with the bottom shelf, mitered at the corners (so it's a 45 degree angle) and beveled on the top edge. Nail this to the two supports. Stack the packing cases, with a little wood glue between them to keep them in place—when the glue's set, you'll secure them using plywood sheets.

To cover the sides, you'll need a piece of plywood for each, cut to the size of the whole side. Secure each one with strips of wood that are 1/4 in. (6 mm) thick and about 1 in. (25 mm) wide, nailed at intervals through the plywood and the packing case so that they form a frame around the edge of each side—a bit like a crude picture frame. Then stand in front of the bookcase and you'll see that the frame, the sheet of ply and the front edge of the packing case itself make an ugly wooden "sandwich." To conceal this you'll need a strip of wood for each front edge, the height of the bookcase and the width of the "sandwich." Nail them in place.

Measure the top and then cut a last piece of 1 in. (25 mm) thick wood so that it can be nailed snugly on the top. Don't bother doing anything to the back—no one's going to see it. Finally, stain and polish the bookcase to finish off.

Fig. 88. *By adding a plinth, you can further disguise the origins of your stylish bookcase.*

56 SCARECROW

Proper scarecrows are rarely seen these days—modern farmers often prefer a loud claxon. This traditional version is a bit quiter, and is ideal for protecting your vegetable patch.

Get a bamboo pole about 10 ft. (3048 mm) long and cut it into two sections—6 ft. (1829 mm) and 4 ft. (1219 mm) long. Bind them into a cross with some twine, crossing them at about 1 ft. (305 mm) down from the top.

Dress it with a shirt so that the cross-piece sticks out of the arms, then stuff it with straw, rags or old clothes. Put the vertical piece of bamboo through the leg of one trouser and tuck in the shirt—the other leg will be fine just hanging there. Tie up the bottom of the trouser legs with rope, stuff them with straw and tie the ends off.

Blow up a balloon for a head and tie it to the top of the bamboo. Paint a face on it and tie on a hat. Stuff long bits of straw or grass under the hat to make hair. Plant the scarecrow firmly into the ground. If you want to scare people as well as birds, use fluorescent paint for the face! The same approach could be used to make a guy.

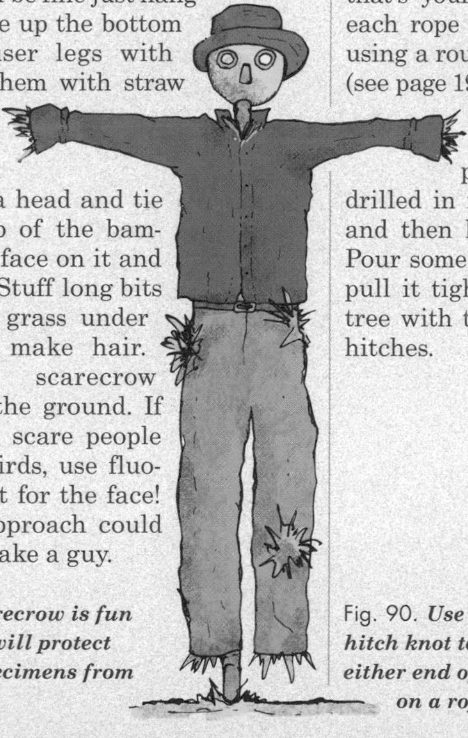

Fig. 89. *A scarecrow is fun to make and will protect your prize specimens from the birds.*

57 ROPE LADDER AND SWING

You don't need a proper ladder to get up into a tree. Instead, make a simple one for yourself out of rope and steps made of hardwood.

The dimensions of the wood depend very much on who's going to be climbing the ladder, so we'll leave that to you. Elsewhere, the secret of the rope ladders is the clove-hitch knot, shown in the diagram. It allows you to create a "hole" into which you can poke the step. Pull the rope tight and the wood is locked into position. Repeat on the other side with a second piece of rope and that's your ladder, Secure the ends of each rope to a stout horizontal bough using a round turn and two half hitches (see page 19).

The swing's even easier. You'll need a bottom-sized piece of board with a hole drilled in it. Thread the rope through and then knot it three or four times. Pour some water on the knot and then pull it tight. Tie the other end to the tree with the round turn and two half hitches.

Fig. 90. *Use the clove-hitch knot to secure either end of each "step" on a rope ladder.*

58 POTTER'S WHEEL

Later on in this book, we'll talk a bit about working with clay, and, although that'll be mostly in the context of models, if you'd like making anything else you'll find this device extremely useful. The whole point of a potter's wheel is that by allowing the raw clay to revolve freely, you'll be able to shape it more effectively, and thus produce better results.

For this you'll need a few basic components and a flat surface at the end to use it on. The base is a simply a piece of hardwood 24 x 11 x 3/4 in. (610 x 279 x 19 mm); to stop it from warping, screw on a couple of battens at each end to act as legs—these should be 11 x 2 x 1 in. (279 x 51 x 25 mm).

The main wheel should be 10 in. (254 mm) in diameter and 3/4 in. (19 mm) thick. Draw this out as accurately as you can—it's important that this circle really is circular—and then drill a hole 1/2 in. (13 mm) deep and no more than 3/16 in. (5 mm) in diameter, making sure that this absolutely does not come through the other side. Cut the circle out using a tenon saw and then sand it to finish. Glue a large cotton reel to the underside of the wheel (making sure its hole

lines up with what you've just drilled) and secure it by nailing in some fine brad nails.

Next, make the smaller, driving wheel from a piece of wood 6 in. (152 mm) in diameter and 1 1/8 in. (30 mm) thick; again, cut it out with a tenon saw and finish with sandpaper. The driving wheel now needs a small handle, so you can turn it with one hand. For this, make a small bore in the wheel—this needs to be 1/2 in. (13 mm) from the edge and big enough to take a small length of dowelling, which forms the handle. Bore down about 1/2 in. (13 mm) into the wood and then glue the dowelling in place.

Measure in 6 in. (152 mm) from the short edge of the base and 5 1/2 in. (140 mm) from the long edge. Make a mark with a pencil. Bore a hole 1/2 in. (13 mm) down into the base big enough to take a short length of dowelling. The exact length of this dowelling (and the screw that you'll need to mount the driving wheel onto the base) will depend on the height of the cotton reel you're using. Essentially, you need to line up the driving wheel with the center of the

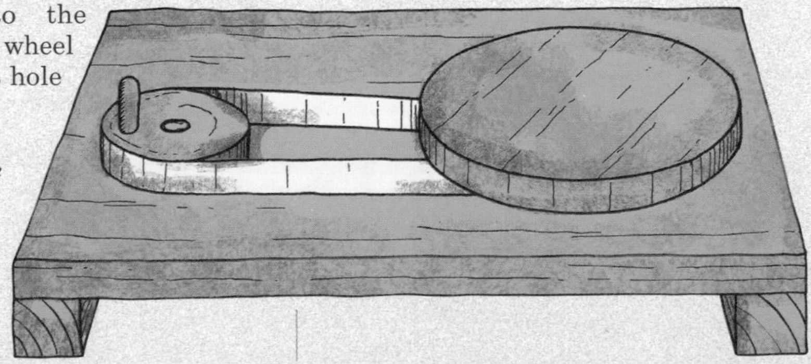

Fig. 91. *A simple potter's wheel like this will help enormously if you fancy making some clay pots.*

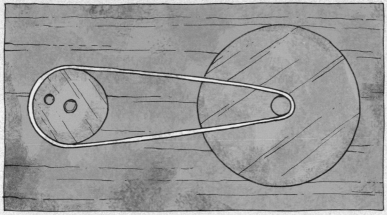

Fig. 92. *You rotate the smaller wheel with one hand and shape the clay with the fingers and thumb of the other.*

cotton reel so that the belt runs parallel to the top of the base—this will ensure that it revolves freely and lets you drive the big wheel by turning the small one. With the dowelling for the big wheel in place, slip a washer over the top and then pop the wheel on top. Make sure it spins freely.

You'll need a large round-headed screw for the driving wheel and another washer. Thread the screw through the top of the driving wheel and then through the washer. Measure in $4^{1}/_{2}$ in. (114 mm) from the short edge and $5^{1}/_{2}$ in. (140 mm) from the long edge and make a pencil mark. Then turn the screw into the base until it reaches the point where the driving wheel is parallel to the center of the cotton reel. Like we said, the exact measurements here will vary slightly depending on the size of the dowelling and screw you've used.

Finally, you'll need a belt of some kind. Canvas is probably the easiest thing to work with—just make sure that it's well sewn where the ends join. Again, you'll need to do some tests to work out the exact length of the belt.

The Secure Shed

SHED LIFE

Thieves are increasingly turning their greedy little eyes in the direction of garden sheds. Even the dumbest burglar can work out that sheds are a soft touch—they're usually sited away from the house, often concealed by trees, and rarely frequented at night. Fight back by doing the following:

- Lock all your tools away after you've used them.
- Lock the shed (and garden gate, if you have one) when you're done.
- Portable, battery-powered alarms work well.
- Keep a note of all valuable tools and mark them with an indelible or ultraviolet pen.
- Check that your home insurance covers things stored in the shed.
- Trim back bushes and trees that may conceal the shed (and thus the person who is breaking into it).
- Consider fitting motion-sensitive night lights.

59 BOX KITE

A box kite like the one illustrated here will fly in the lightest winds and can be put together for some loose change. These measurements are for a 5 ft. (1524 mm) high kite, but you can change the overall size to suit yourself, so long as you keep the altered measurements in proportion.

To build this one, though, you basically need three bamboo "boxes" 30 x 20 in. (762 x 508 mm) covered in light lawncloth. You'll need to fit the three sections to corner bamboo struts, gluing the cloth over all the edges and then taping it to stop it from stretching.

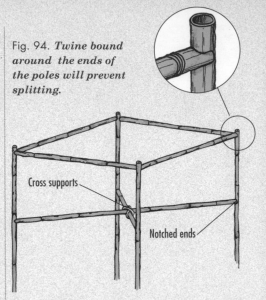

Fig. 94. *Twine bound around the ends of the poles will prevent splitting.*

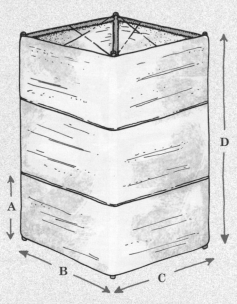

A = 20 in. (508 mm)
B = 30 in. (762 mm)
C = 30 in. (762 mm)
D = 5 ft. (1524 mm)

Fig. 93. *Wires are fixed across the frame to add bracing.*

Although it's called a "box" kite, it's actually more of a diamond shape, and if you look at the kite on its end you'll see that two of the angles are 60 degrees and that the other two are 120 degrees. Make small pockets at the ends of the cloth to fit the bamboo sticks in to and then add interior cross supports to help the kite keep its shape; these cross-pieces are notched at each end to fit into the corner posts, and bound in the middle. Another useful trick is to bind each crosspiece just before the end—to stop it from splitting.

In use, the kite may twist out of shape unless you incorporate some wires stretched from two of the corners to the center of the opposite side, as shown in Fig. 93. You can also run longer cords from top to bottom and from corner to corner.

Tie the flying cord to a bamboo stick about 24 in. (610 mm) from one of the wide corners. There's no "best" point at which to tie it on—you'll just have to try it and see.

60 CHILDREN'S PICNIC TABLE

This is one of the easiest, most useful projects you'll ever make—and boys and girls will love it.

If you can get the timber cut and finished down to the following sizes, you won't have to do so much yourself and you'll waste less wood. Here's what you need: four legs of 22 x 2³/4 x ³/4 in. (555 x 65 x 20 mm); two tabletop supports of 16¹/2 x 2³/4 x ³/4 in. (420 x 65 x 20 mm); two seat supports of 33 x 2³/4 x ³/4 in. (840 x 65 x 20 mm); one brace of 24¹/2 x 2³/4 x ³/4 in. (620 x 65 x 20 mm); three boards for the tabletop of 35¹/2 x 5¹/2 x ³/4 in. (900 x 140 x 20 mm); and two seat boards of 35¹/2 x 5¹/2 x ³/4 in. (900 x 140 x 20 mm). Tell your supplier that it's going to be used outside so they can advise you which wood will be best.

OK, first angle the ends of the four legs to 30 degrees, parallel to each other (i.e., so they both slope in the same direction!); you can also trim the bottom corners off the seat and the tabletop supports, though this is purely decorative and you don't have to.

Fig. 95 gives you all the measurements you need, so start by putting the crosspieces 2 and 3 flat on the floor and then place two of the legs (1) on top of them in the correct position, securing them with a 1¹/2 in. (38 mm) woodscrew wherever the legs and crosspieces meet. Get someone to help you stand the completed ends up and then position and screw the brace (4) into place between them using two screws at each end—the brace needs to be exactly in the middle of the two top end pieces (2).

Add the two seat boards and the three tabletop boards; make sure they're positioned symmetrically and screw them in place. Treat the wood if you need to but make sure it's completely dry before you use it.

A = 16¹/2 in. (420 mm)
B = 33 in. (840 mm)
C = 8 in. (200 mm)
D = 11 in. (280 mm)

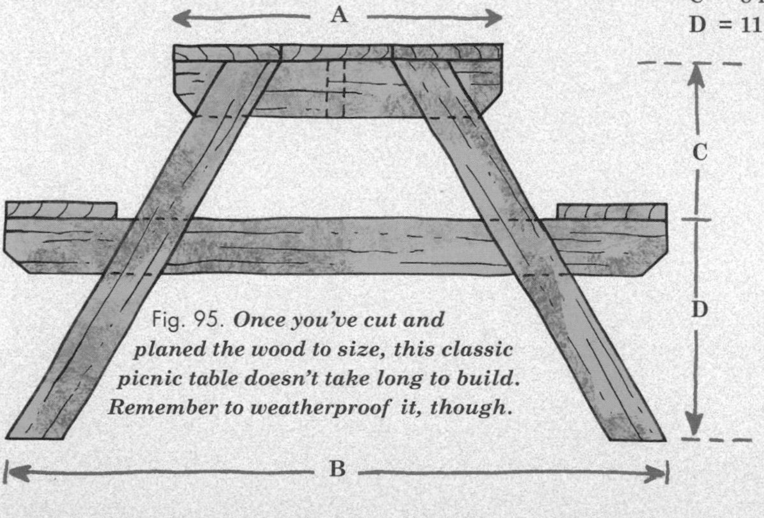

Fig. 95. *Once you've cut and planed the wood to size, this classic picnic table doesn't take long to build. Remember to weatherproof it, though.*

61 A HOMEMADE "TELESCOPE"

Although this doesn't look like a telescope—it's not in a tube—it will show you quite clearly how a real one works. All you need are a pair of weak reading glasses of the kind you can buy in drug store without prescription (or from a yard sale), a magnifying glass, a flashlight, some gaffer tape, some waxed paper, and someone to help you.

Take the reading glasses, open them, and tape one of the lenses to the upright part of a chair—this should leave the other lens poking out from the side of the chair. Put the flashlight on a flat surface about 13 ft. (4 m) away from the glasses' lens, then turn it on. Adjust the position (you may have to put it on some books or something similar) until it's shining on the lens.

Go to the other side of the glasses, take the waxed paper and hold it in front of the lens like a miniature movie screen. Walk slowly away from the lens, still holding up the paper, until you see an image of the flashlight on the paper. Now you need a friend. Get them to hold the paper where it is while you go around the back—this means you now have a "line" of objects that goes flashlight, lens, paper and then you.

Take the magnifying glass and look at the image on the paper—move the glass back and forth until the image appears magnified. Then tell your friend to take the paper away. Without the wax paper to diffuse the light, the image of the flashlight should be much brighter and easier to see. You can also get your friend to place some other objects near to the flashlight, then look at them

through the magnifying glass by moving it up and down and from side to side. When you've had a go, swap places with your friend and repeat the experiment.

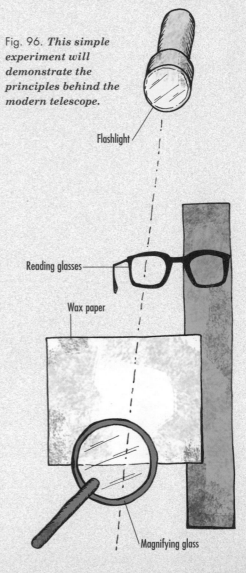

Fig. 96. *This simple experiment will demonstrate the principles behind the modern telescope.*

Flashlight

Reading glasses

Wax paper

Magnifying glass

62 PIGGY BANK

You can make this neat piggy bank from a few bits and pieces, most of which will be lying around the house. The clever bit? Using the balloon as a mold for the shape.

First, decide how large you want the piggy bank to be (how much money have you got?), blow up the balloon to that size and tie it off. Then cut some newspaper into scraps or strips. You'll have to guess the quantity at the start, but you can always make more. To make the paste, you'll need two cups of hot water, a large bowl and a couple of cups of white flour. Mix everything together until it's lump-free. Coat the paper on both sides with the paste and then lay it over the balloon, working in the same direction until it's covered—don't forget to leave a gap to put the money in. Add another layer in a different direction and then a third in yet another. Let it dry.

Use the cardboard from a toilet paper roll to make the pig's feet and ears. You should cover all these with papier maché and leave them to dry.

When everything's ready, take a pin and stick it through the slot to pop the balloon, then use the pin to pull out the burst balloon. Paint everything with white acrylic, and when that's dry you can use a more pig-like color for the body, feet and nose. When they're dry, stick them onto the body.

The only drawback with this piggy bank is that you'll have to smash it to get the money out!

Fig. 97. *The piggy bank is the sort of project you can do with a young child.*

The Shed Survey

A survey conducted in 2003 revealed that around 52 percent of people regularly go to their sheds for some peace and quiet or to make stuff; this group is almost equally divided among men and women. Nearly a quarter of the people surveyed admitted to using their sheds for something other than traditional DIY or gardening, and six percent said they'd seriously considered transforming their shed into a pub. All this in the year that Britons spent an estimated £85m on sheds.

63 MATCHSTICK MODELS, TIPS AND TRICKS

The world of matchstick modeling is an extraordinary one, full of miniature marvels packed with detail and assembled with care and painstaking precision. However, it's not necessarily a world you'd want to jump straight into.

If you decide to take up jigsaw puzzles, for example, it's probably best not to start with a 5,000 piece picture of the Sahara; similarly, although matchstick-model kits of the Taj Mahal or London Bridge may look fantastic, they're just as likely to put you off if you're a first-timer. Instead, find out if you're a matchstick kind of person by trying this self-standing building block. Although it looks simple, it uses many of the principles of layering and locking that allow you to produce models that hold together without needing any glue.

All you need is a flat surface, a large box of household matches and a steady hand. If it turns out that you have problems in keeping the tower of matches correctly positioned, skip to the end

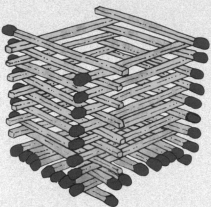

Fig. 99. *Add extra layers as shown, taking note of how the match heads are arranged.*

and see how to secure them first using a board and four nails. Otherwise, if you're feeling confident, read on.

Start by placing two matches on the table. They should be parallel, just under a match length apart, with the heads facing the same way. Next, take eight matches and lay them across the first two; they should be evenly spaced, with the match heads and tails protruding slightly at either end; all the match heads should point in the same direction. Now lay another layer of eight matches on top of those. Again the heads and tails should protrude slightly and all the heads should be facing the same way—see Fig. 98.

Now you have to build up the "walls." Each layer is made up of two matches whose match heads point in opposite directions. So, if you're looking at the model and the second layer of eight matches have their heads pointing

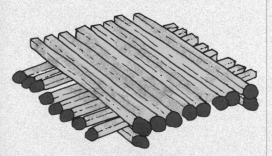

Fig. 98. *Start with two matches, and then add two layers on top of them like this.*

toward you, the first match goes on the edge nearest to you, head pointing left; the next match goes on the back with the head pointing right. On top of these, place a third match on the left side with the head pointing away from you and a fourth on the right-hand side with the head pointing toward you. Carrying on building the walls until you have seven layers in all—see Fig. 99.

Fig. 100. *Slot the matches down through the structure. The coin will help keep them in place.*

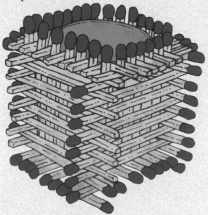

OK, next you need to place a layer of eight matches on top of the walls—making sure that the heads are all pointing in the same direction, but opposite to those on the "floor" at the bottom of the tower. Now add a further layer of six matches, heads all pointing in the same direction, but laid closer together so there's more space either side of them—they basically need to be the width of a small coin apart.

Place a coin on top of the tower and then gently insert a matchstick vertically into the space at one corner. You'll need to jiggle it around a little—care-

fully—but you should be able to push it all the way down until it engages with the equivalent corner at the bottom of the tower. Do the same at the other four corners, threading each match carefully as before.

This is the really tricky bit. You now have to work your way around the top of the box, threading matches vertically down through all the gaps in the top two levels so that they engage with the equivalent matches on the bottom two levels. Work your way round the top until it looks like Fig. 100.

Now you can take the coin out—very carefully—with a spare matchstick. When you've done that, secure the box by pressing gently in on all the sides to make sure the matches mesh together as they should, and you've got a free-standing box—Fig. 101.

If you simply can't keep the tower steady enough to build it, get a block of wood and lay your first level of matches on it, then knock four nails into the wood at each corner. This will help to stabilize the tower.

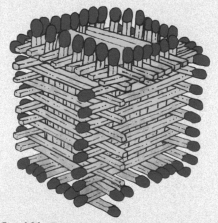

Fig. 101. *Remove the coin and gently press in all the matches so they lock into a single solid structure.*

Matchstick Modeling tips

The most important attribute that any matchstick modeller needs is patience, pure and simple. Rome will not be built in a day—and certainly not if it's made of 4000 matchsticks—so pace yourself. While you're learning not to rush things, you'll also learn that it's best not to try and model when you're tired. This is difficult work at the best of times, and your model will suffer if you're not feeling alert and sharp. You certainly don't want to have to go back and fix something you got wrong an hour ago—it's a bit like having to unpick stitches, only much harder.

If you're building a commercial matchstick model from a kit, follow the instructions carefully—you'll learn lots of useful techniques along the way that will help you become a better model maker. For example, some kits come with precut card shapes for you to glue the matches onto, you should always apply the glue with a brush to the card, rather than to the individual matches; similarly, you should always allow plenty of time for the glue to dry and press flat sections down under something like a book.

One of the real skills of matchstick modeling is the ability to make unusual shapes from the matches. For example, if you need to make an octagon, try and find an octagonal object of the right size and then wrap it in paper, glued at the edge. You can then glue the matches in a circle round the paper. When they've dried, you can remove the paper sleeve from the object and you've got your hexagon of matches. It's also possible to bend individual matches just by soaking them in water overnight—after that, with care you can bend them into the required shapes.

Another useful trick will help you to build large flat surfaces quickly and easily. All you need to do is to glue the matches to a sheet of Perspex and then let it dry for at least a couple of days. Afterwards, you'll find that you can gently peel the matches away from the Perspex quite easily—the matches however, will stay stuck together, like a miniature wall.

Although a craft knife will do the job—assuming you've got a good cutting surface—you'll also find it useful to have a dedicated cutter, which you can buy from a hobby shop; a little bowl of water and hand towel are also good for getting rid of excess glue.

Other tools that you'll find handy include G-clamps, scissors, a small pair of pliers, a ruler and some sandpaper—fine and coarse; some model makers swear by those emery boards used for filing and shaping fingernails. And for a change of shape, consider using toothpicks alongside matches for interesting changes in texture.

Finally, a clean and tidy space to work in is important—but of course you do that anyway, right?

64 A Cotton-Reel Car

For this you'll need an ordinary cotton reel, a small nail (smaller than the diameter of the reel), a rubber band, a stick about 3⁷/₈ to 5⁷/₈ in. (100–150 mm) long and a slice of candle with a hole in the middle. Fit them together as follows.

Make a groove across one end of the cotton reel with a fretsaw or something that lets you make precise cuts. It should only be deep enough so that the little nail lays snugly in the groove. Thread the rubber band through the hole in the center of the cotton reel, pop the nail through the band loop and pull the band back so the nail sits in the groove. Slip the candle slice over the other end of the rubber band and then put the stick through the band loop. Twist the stick around until the rubber band is tight, put it down on a flat surface and it'll shoot off.

Obviously, the rubber band powers the "car," but the key component is the slice of candle, which reduces the friction. Replace the stick with a lolly stick and you can make a handy little personal fan! Just watch it doesn't fly off and hit you in the eye.

Fig. 102.
Turn the stick to wind the elastic. When you let go, your "car" will trundle off.

65 Magic Tops

OK, so they're not really magic, but these simple tops can teach you a lot about how your eyes see shapes and colors. All you need is some white card and some black ink—the blacker the better. Start by tracing around the two designs shown here, and then copy the results onto your card. Carefully fill in any shapes with an ink pen and then set aside to dry.

When the ink's dry, cut around the circle shape and make a hole in the middle. You can use an old pencil for the spindle or any other suitably shaped piece of wood that you have to hand. It shouldn't be longer than 2 in. (51 mm) long, though.

Try spinning the first top (with the star design) and watch what happens to the pattern—it should look completely black in the middle and then start to fade the nearer it gets to the edge. The saw pattern will produce a set of circles, very dark at the center of the top and then lighter the closer you get to the edge. This is all down to what's called the persistence of vision, and happens it whenever we look at a fast-moving or quickly spinning object.

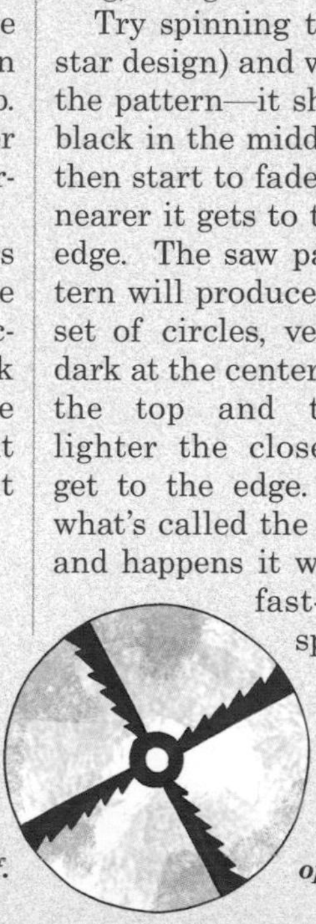

Fig. 103.
Even simple patterns can create exciting optical illusions.

66 MINI SCOOTER

This has an advantage over most basic toy scooters in that you can steer it—and it's got a brake!

You'll need the following lengths of pine: two pieces of 30 x 1 1/2 x 1 1/4 in. (762 x 38 x 32 mm); one piece of 10 x 2 1/2 x 1 1/2 in. (254 x 63.5 x 38 mm); one piece of 32 x 1 1/2 x 1 1/4 in. (813 x 38 x 32 mm); and one piece of 12 x 1 1/2 x 1 1/4 in. (305 x 38 x 32 mm).

You'll need the following assorted bolts as well: two eye bolts 2 x 1/4 in. (51 x 6 mm) with a 5/8 in. (16 mm) hole; two eye bolts 3 x 1/4 in. (76 x 6 mm) with a 5/8 in. (16 mm) hole; four 1 3/4 x 1/4 in. (44 x 6 mm) coach bolts; two 1 3/4 x 1/4 in. (44 x 6 mm) hexagonal head bolts; six 2 3/4 x 1/4 in. (70 x 6 mm) coach bolts; two 5 x 1/2 in. (127 x 13 mm) coach bolts; two 6 x 1/2 in. (152 x 13 mm) hexagonal head bolts; one 8 x 1/2 in. (203 x 13 mm) coach bolt; along with 20 washers and 20 nuts. Finally, you'll need three wheels 4 in. (102 mm) in diameter, with a 1/2 in. (13 mm) hole in the middle and a center thickness of 1 1/2 in. (38 mm); three 2 x 2 in. (51 x 51 mm) brackets; four eye bolts; and one T-shaped hinge.

Use the plan on these pages to cut the wood out to the correct size. If you want to improve the cosmetics, you can round the edges of the footplate and cut an

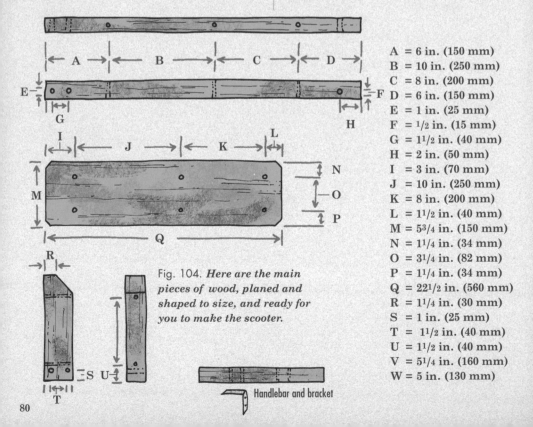

Fig. 104. *Here are the main pieces of wood, planed and shaped to size, and ready for you to make the scooter.*

Handlebar and bracket

A = 6 in. (150 mm)
B = 10 in. (250 mm)
C = 8 in. (200 mm)
D = 6 in. (150 mm)
E = 1 in. (25 mm)
F = 1/2 in. (15 mm)
G = 1 1/2 in. (40 mm)
H = 2 in. (50 mm)
I = 3 in. (70 mm)
J = 10 in. (250 mm)
K = 8 in. (200 mm)
L = 1 1/2 in. (40 mm)
M = 5 3/4 in. (150 mm)
N = 1 1/4 in. (34 mm)
O = 3 1/4 in. (82 mm)
P = 1 1/4 in. (34 mm)
Q = 22 1/2 in. (560 mm)
R = 1 1/4 in. (30 mm)
S = 1 in. (25 mm)
T = 1 1/2 in. (40 mm)
U = 1 1/2 in. (40 mm)
V = 5 1/4 in. (160 mm)
W = 5 in. (130 mm)

angle into the neck—if not, you can just leave them squared off. Most of the holes you'll need to drill are 1/4 in. (6 mm)—the exceptions are those for the axle bolts and the one that attaches the runners to the neck, which are all 1/2 in. (12 mm).

Start by putting the front wheels on. One of the 1/2 in. (12 mm) bolts makes the axle with a washer between the upright and each wheel; pop the wheels on and then use two nuts at either end, tightening one against the other to lock it. Screw the two eyeholes in place in the upright as indicated on the plan, and then add the actual handlebars by bolting the two angle brackets to the top of the upright and then attaching the bar to them with two bolts on each side.

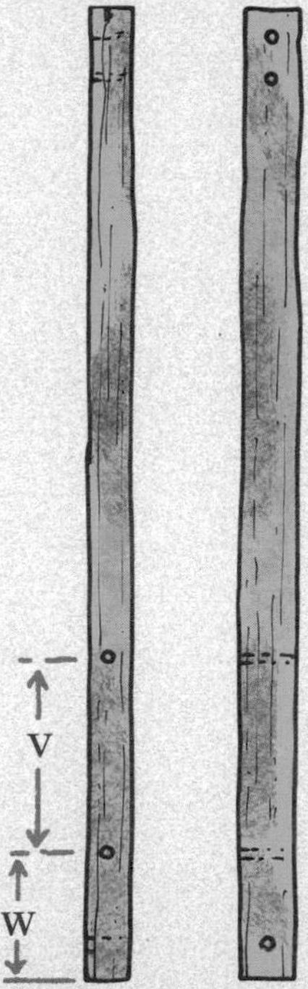

Lay the two runners parallel to each other and attach them to the neck with two of the larger bolts; then screw the other two eye bolts into the short neck piece as shown in the plan. Then bolt the running plate to the two runners with six coach bolts.

Use an angle bracket and four screws to attach the short neck to the top of the running plate, then line up the eye bolts on the short neck piece and the upright (it may help if a friend does this).

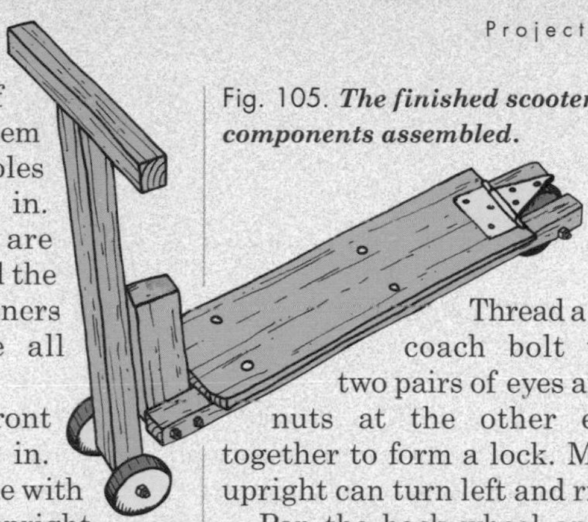

Fig. 105. *The finished scooter with all the components assembled.*

Single back wheel

Thread a 1/2 in. (12 mm) coach bolt through the two pairs of eyes and, using two nuts at the other end, tighten together to form a lock. Make sure the upright can turn left and right properly.

Pop the back wheel on in the same way as you attached the front pair, then attach the hinge to the back of the scooter with three screws so that it rubs against the wheel when you press down on it, acting as a brake.

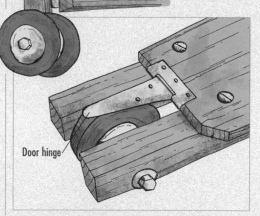

Fig. 106. *A simple hinge mechanism allows you to steer the scooter by turning the handlebar.*

Metal rod

Door hinge

Fig. 107. *A door hinge makes a highly effective brake—just step on it to slow the scooter down.*

67 BAGATELLE BOARD

Bagatelle is a bit like pinball. You use a spring plunger to fire a little ball out onto the board and then score points depending on whether it goes down one of the holes or ends up in one of the channels—each are marked with different scores.

Although it's pretty straightforward to make, the bagatelle board requires a bit of a shopping list. Here goes: you'll need a base of 24 1/2 x 12 x 1/2 in. (622 x 305 x 13 mm) plywood; two sides of 25 x 2 1/4 x 1/2 in. (635 x 63.5 x 13 mm); one top end measuring 13 x 2 1/4 x 1/2 in. (330 x 63.5 x 13 mm); one bottom end of 13 x 1 3/4 x 1/2 in. (330 x 44 x 13 mm); two long channel dividers of 16 x 1 1/4 x 3/8 in. (406 x 32 x 11 mm); two medium ones of 6 x 1 1/4 x 3/8 in. (152 x 32 x 11 mm); two short ones of 4 x 1 1/4 x 3/8 in. (102 x 32 x 11 mm); and plywood measuring 21 x 1 1/4 x 1/8 in. (533 x 32 x 11 mm). (Note that all these measurements are for wood that's been planed to size and cleaned up. If you're going to do that yourself, adjust the sizes accordingly.) You can see the finished plan, with measurements, in the main diagram on the facing page.

You can simply nail the box together at the corners or make a stronger version with dovetail joints—use a single dovetail at the narrow corners and two at the other end. Before you do, remember that the top end is 1/2 in. (13 mm) higher than the bottom, so you'll have to plane the sides so that they're 2 1/4 in. (63.5 mm) high at the top and only 1 3/4 in. (44.5 mm) at the bottom. Then, cut out the dovetails as shown in

Fig. 108. Sand the inside of the box and glue the four sides together.

Take the plywood base and see if it fits in the box—if not, plane the edges until it does. Then screw it into the position shown, with round-headed brass screws, making sure that it's at the angle shown; it needs to be sloped so that any balls which don't fall down one of the holes will roll back into one of the channels.

Next you need a semicircular top, about 1 1/4 in. (32 mm) high and made from either sheet metal or thin plywood. Make sure the top of the curve touches the edge and then notch the two ends into the side before screwing them into position with countersunk screws—two at the top and two at each end.

Work out what you're going to use as a ball – marbles or ball bearings work fine – decide where you want to put the holes, then drill them down to about 5/16 in. (9 mm), making sure they're slightly bigger than the balls.

A = 2 1/4 in. (57 mm)
B = 1 3/4 in. (44.5 mm)
C = 13 in. (330 mm)
D = 3 in. (76 mm)
E = 1 1/4 in. (32 mm)
F = 1 1/2 in. (38 mm)
G = 1 1/2 in. (38 mm)
H = 1 1/2 in. (38 mm)
I = 1 1/2 in. (38 mm)
J = 1 1/2 in. (38 mm)
K = 1 1/4 in. (32 mm)
L = 1 1/4 in. (32 mm)
M = 1 in. (25 mm)
N = 1/2 in. (13 mm)

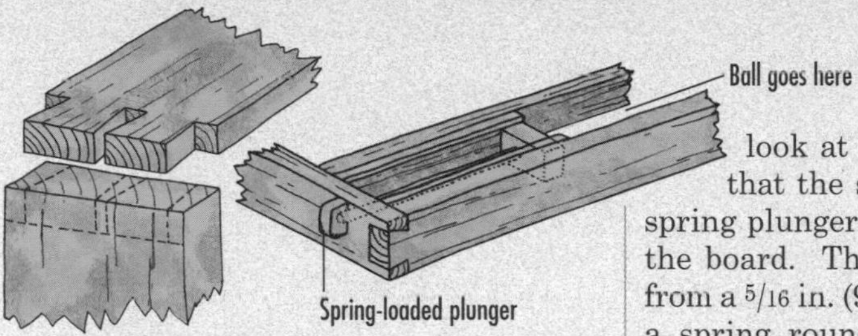

Ball goes here

Spring-loaded plunger

Fig. 108. *Marking out the dovetail joints on the sides and top of the board.*

Take your channel dividers and round one long edge, then pin them from under the plywood board and at the end. You can see their exact position if you

look at the diagram—make sure that the strip that will house the spring plunger is parallel to the side of the board. The plunger itself is made from a $5/16$ in. (9 mm) hardwood rod with a spring round it. Although you can make the spring yourself from stiff wire—like piano wire—it's easier to use a store-bought one. Overall, the spring plunger should be between 4 to 5 in. (102 and 127 mm) long. One end should be glued into a block of hardwood $11/4$ x 1 x $1/2$ in.(32 x 25 x 13 mm). Slide the block and spring plunger into the channel and mark where the other end touches the end of the board. Drill a hole here, pass the end of the plunger through and then glue a handle onto the end. Now, when you pull the handle back, the spring plunger and block end will come with it. Place a marble in the channel, let go of the handle, and it'll fly round the board. If you have problems with the plunger rising up, glue and pin a pair of wooden guides 6 x $1/4$ x $1/4$ in. (152 x 6 x 6 mm) above it, 1 in.(25 mm) above the base. If the guides generate too much friction, rub a lead pencil over them.

Finally, nail in $11/4$ in. (32 mm) panel pins to give your marble something to bounce off—leave about $7/8$ in. (23 mm) of each one sticking out—and then number the holes and the channels and use these to score the game.

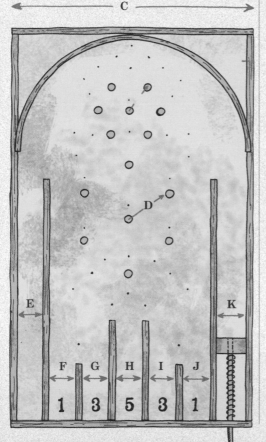

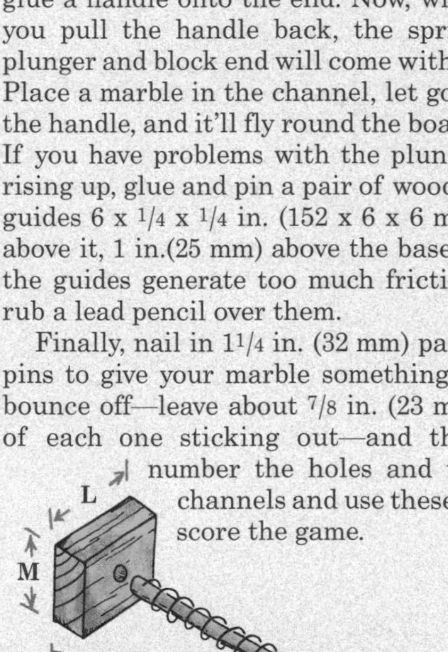

C

D

E   K

F G H I J

1 3 5 3 1

L

M

N

Fig. 109. *The plunger is made from a wooden rod wrapped in a spring.*

68 A HOUSE NAMEPLATE

There are many different kinds of nameplates you can create in wood or metal—this combines the two and is designed to be hung over the front door. The design shown uses copper for the metal letters and a hardwood back; something like oak will work well.

You'll need a sheet of 16 gauge copper (as copper goes, this is fairly thick, so you may want to practice on a spare bit before trying the real thing). Make sure you leave enough space top and bottom for six holes (two on the top and bottom edges and one at either end) to secure the metal sign to the back board.

To cut the letters out you'll first need to drill a small hole so you can fit a saw through—you can use a hacksaw for this, but it's better and more precise to work with a fretsaw fitted with a blade that's able to cut metal. When the letters are complete, clean up any rough edges with a smooth file. Polish the finished sign to give it a good shine.

Cut a piece of oak—or other dark wood suitable for use outdoors—slightly larger all round than the metal sign and then chisel and sand the ends so they're nice and rounded. Screw the

The Shed Connected

There are certain must-have fixtures in a shed. Traditionally, these were things like a workbench and stool, perhaps an oil lamp or, if you were particularly flashy, electric power. Now it's the Internet, and, if the story of one Stephen Riley from Lancashire is anything to go by, you'd better take it seriously. As Mr. Riley stayed late in his shed, absorbed with surfing the Net, fun-seeking locals decided to lock him in. When no one heard his cries for help—it was by now 4:00 A.M. — he posted a message on a website, asking if whoever read it would contact the local police. His electronic cry for help was heard by a concerned chatroom visitor in the U.S., who promptly called the Lancashire constabulary. Once persuaded that it wasn't a joke, they went around and freed Mr. Riley.

sign onto the wood and then add two screw rings on the top edge to hang it. Signs made in this style actually get better with age, acquiring a nice, weather-beaten look.

Fig. 110. *You'll need a fretsaw fitted with a metal-cutting blade to make the letters for your house nameplate.*

69 TIN-CAN TELEPHONE

70 THE JUMPING COIN

This is a classic that's still worth making, and all you need are two tin cans and a bit of string. First, remove any sharp edges from your cans and then wash them out. Dry both thoroughly. Take a hammer and nail or a screwdriver (or indeed anything you can use to punch through the can) and make a hole in the bottom of each tin.

This is a great trick, but be careful— that coin really does jump!

Get an empty glass bottle and stick it in the freezer. Leave it there for about an hour—or until it's good and cold. Take it out of the freezer and wipe a damp cloth over the top to make it wet. Then, take a small coin and completely cover the open top of the bottle—if air can get in or out, the trick won't work.

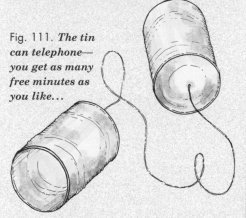

Fig. 111. *The tin can telephone— you get as many free minutes as you like…*

Now, rub your hands together quickly 20 times and then cover the sides of the bottle with them. Make sure everyone else keeps their distance, and make sure to point the bottle away from you. The coin will "jump" off the top of the bottle. This works because heat makes things expand—in this case, the air in the bottle—and because the air can't escape at first, the pressure on the coin increases until it shoots up into the air.

Take one end of the string—it can be up to 10 ft. (3,048 mm) long—and thread it through the hole. Tie a couple of good knots to stop it slipping back through. Repeat with the can at the other end.

One person should stick their ear to the open end of one can while the other person talks into the open end of the other can. The trick to getting a good sound is to make sure you keep the string between the two cans taut. As the first person speaks, the string between the cans vibrates—and that's what the second person hears.

Fig. 112. *Make sure the bottle is nice and cold before you take it from the freezer—then ensure that the coin sits tightly on the top before you start the trick.*

⑦ MODEL AIRPLANES

This traditionally styled glider is fully capable of flying for nearly 100 meters thanks to a clever and simple design. You can make the main body from a single piece of something like silver spruce, 36 in. (914 mm) long and 3/8 in. (10 mm) square. Next, use some 16 SWG (standard wire gauge) wire to bind a weight onto the nose—something like a 2 oz. (56.6 g) piece of lead will do fine.

Use 18 SWG wire to shape the rudder so that it's about 4¹/2 in. (114 mm) from top to bottom and 3¹/2 in. (89 mm) from front to back. To cover this in the traditional way, lay it on top of a piece of silk and cut around the shape, leaving a small margin. Use scissors to make little cuts in the margin and then glue it around the rudder; wait until the glue's tacky, then fix one side completely before pulling the silk gently taut and fixing the other side.

Next, drill a hole in the fuselage about 1 in. (25 mm) from the tail end, then poke the rudder prong into the hole and bind it firmly with thread; then fix it with a drop of solder. The tail is made from birch 3/8 x 1/16 in. (10 x 2 mm) square to the dimensions shown in Fig. 115, and then glued and nailed. You'll also need a 3/8 x 3/8 x 3/16 in. (10 x 10 x 6 mm) block, which fits between the fuselage and the tail spar, as shown in Fig. 113. The idea here is to lift the back

end of the tail by about 3/16 in. (5 mm). Cover the tail fin in the same way as you did the rudder and then bind it to the fuselage with thread.

If you look at Fig. 115, you'll see not only the outline of the tail but also of the main wing. This is also made from birch; you'll need 3/8 x 1/8 in. (10 x 3 mm) lengths for the long spars and 3/8 x 1/16 in. (10 x 2 mm) lengths for the short ones. See Fig. 115 for the rest of the dimensions and notice that the central spar (where the wing crosses the fuselage) actually extends from the wing by about 1 in. (25 mm) at either end; note too that this should be made of 3/8 x 1/8 in. (10 x 3 mm), the same as the long spars. The joints for the wing section should be glued and nailed—use a fine bradawl to prepare the holes first.

Here's a good trick. You want to introduce a gentle convex curve to the wing, because it'll help to keep the glider in the air for longer. With the wing frame complete and all the glue dried, boil some water and then hold the wing frame over the steam so it plays onto the short spars, about one third of the way from the front down each one. Bend each spar gently under the steam. This is a tricky procedure but what you're trying to do is a put a curve into the wing that lifts it about 3/8 in. (10 mm) from the horizontal; try to get exactly the same curve in each spar.

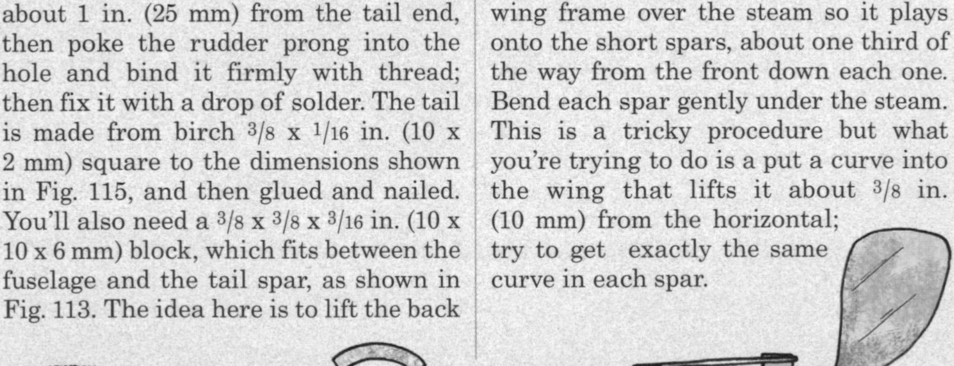

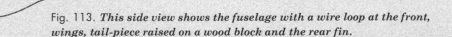

Fig. 113. *This side view shows the fuselage with a wire loop at the front, wings, tail-piece raised on a wood block and the rear fin.*

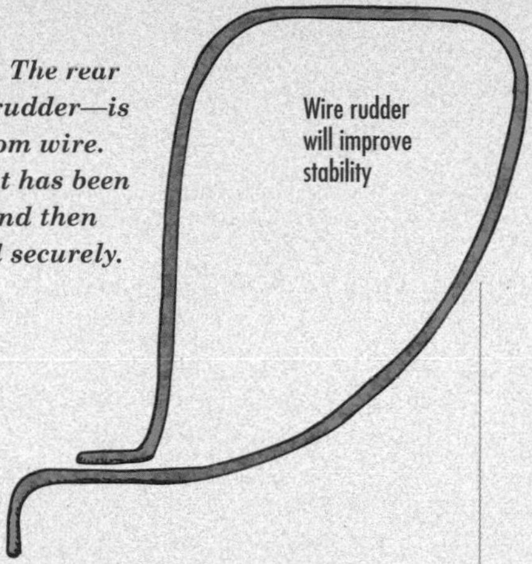

Fig. 114. *The rear fin—or rudder—is made from wire. The joint has been bound and then soldered securely.*

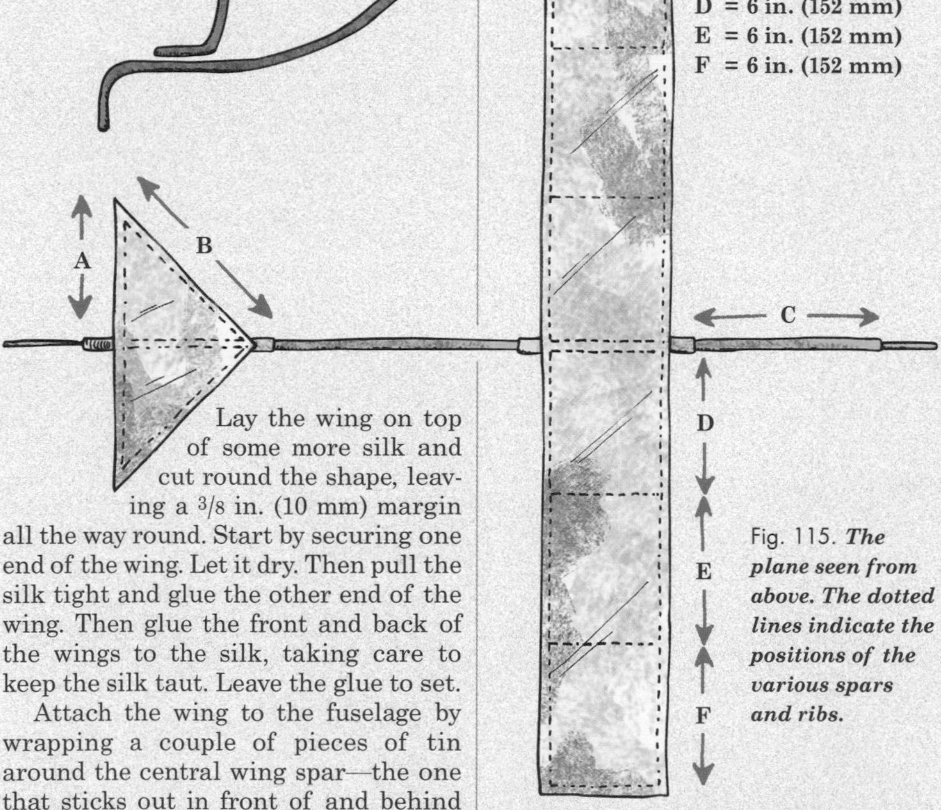

Wire rudder will improve stability

A = 6 in. (152 mm)
B = 10$^{1/2}$ in. (267 mm)
C = 6 in. (152 mm)
D = 6 in. (152 mm)
E = 6 in. (152 mm)
F = 6 in. (152 mm)

A

B

C

D

Fig. 115. *The plane seen from above. The dotted lines indicate the positions of the various spars and ribs.*

E

F

Lay the wing on top of some more silk and cut round the shape, leaving a $^{3/8}$ in. (10 mm) margin all the way round. Start by securing one end of the wing. Let it dry. Then pull the silk tight and glue the other end of the wing. Then glue the front and back of the wings to the silk, taking care to keep the silk taut. Leave the glue to set.

Attach the wing to the fuselage by wrapping a couple of pieces of tin around the central wing spar—the one that sticks out in front of and behind the wing—and make sure these are tight enough to stay put, but also not so tight that you can't slide the wing up and down the fuselage a bit if you need to. Then fix both with a drop of solder, so they're like little metal sleeves over the projecting spar. Then try balancing the plane on the tip of your finger—by moving the wing up and down the fuselage, you should be able to find the correct point of balance. Then, when you try flying the plane, watch what happens. If the plane nosedives into the ground, move the wing forward slightly if it rises quickly, move it backward a little bit.

72 A WORM HOTEL

When the worm hotel is up and running it will serve two purposes. First, the one described here will compost food scraps for an average family; and second, it'll provide a good source of bait for anyone who goes fishing.

Building the hotel involves hardly any building at all. All you need is a box 35¹/₂ x 23¹/₂ x 11³/₄ in. (900 x 600 x 300 mm) preferably made of wood. Although you can use plastic, wood is more absorbent and will keep the worms nice and warm. Don't use a metal container, as it may contaminate the compost.

Give the box a good cleaning and then knock out some ³/₈ in. (10 mm) holes all over the bottom and the sides. This is for drainage. Raise it on bricks—this

lets you put a tray underneath to catch any excess water. You can use ordinary sheets of newspaper to line the inside and then you should half-fill it with well-rotted compost—make sure it's nice and damp. If you can't get compost, then soaked, shredded newspaper or cardboard mixed with earth will do nearly as well. You can also enrich the hotel's insides by adding leaves, straw, peat and so on.

To kick off a wormery this size you'll need between 500 and 1,000 worms. Patient wormers can dig these up themselves; impatient ones can get them in bulk via mailorder. Once the worms are in, cover the top with newspaper or hessian to keep the light out and the damp in, then cover completely with a lid that's tight enough to keep animals and the rain out.

If you start with approximately 17¹/₂ oz. (500 g) of vegetable scraps in the first week, you can then add more week by week as the worm population increases. Check every few days to see if the newspaper/hessian on the top is damp and, if it isn't, add some water. If all goes well, you should have ten times as many worms within the year.

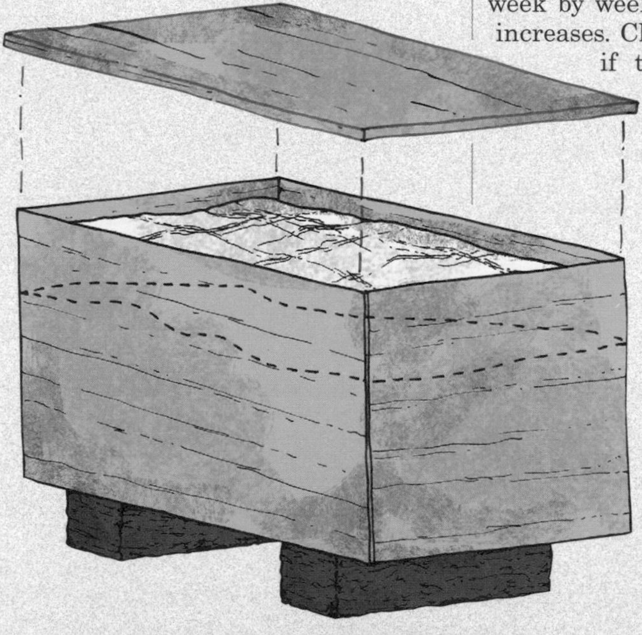

Fig. 116. *A wooden box is warmer and more absorbent than a metal one, but either will provide an environment in which your worms can get composting.*

88

73 PACKING-CASE DESK

If you can get good ones, wooden packing cases are excellent building blocks for various items of furniture. We've already seen how to make a bookcase (page 68)—here's how you can make a useful writing desk.

Decorate with beading

The desktop frame

You'll require four packing cases and a framed top covered with plywood. The cases need to be of the same dimensions—preferably 18 x 12 in. (457 x 305 mm)—and as deep as you can find them. You should leave a gap between the two sets of cases of about 18 in. (457 mm) so you've got enough room for your knees. Instead of drawers—which are more complicated—this version uses hinged doors that "fall" open.

To conceal the desk's origins, cover each side with a piece of plywood cut to size. Secure each side with strips of wood that are 1/4 in. (6 mm) thick and about 1 in. (25 mm) wide, nailed at intervals through the plywood and case to form a frame around the edge of each side. For decorative purposes, you can add a cross in the center of each side made from ordinary batten.

Raise each stack of packing cases by nailing two supports to the bottom as a stand—make them about 1 in. (25 mm) wide and between 2 in. (51 mm) and 3 in. (76 mm) high. Make a plinth for each lower packing case about 1 in. (25 mm) thick and high enough to reach the bottom of the case; miter the corners

to 45-degree angles and bevel the top edge. Then nail them to the supports.

You can use plywood as the front for each door, supported by a frame of wood on the inside, secured by corrugated steel fasteners and hinged with two hinges. For the top of the desk, make a frame from 2 x 1 in. (51 x 25 mm) wood (make sure you put a piece across the middle) and then cover it with plywood, cut to leave a 1/4 in. (6 mm) gap around the edge. Use beading to fill the gap and decorate the desktop.

*Fig. 117. **Two packing cases per side, framed on the top and then covered with plywood, is all that it takes to build this handsome homemade desk.***

74 MATCHBOX DISPENSER

Designed to hold 12 boxes of safety matches, this little dispenser makes a neat addition to any kitchen. A fine-grained wood like white holly or sycamore will work best for both the body and the overlay— these are made of 3/16 in. (5 mm) and 1/8 in. (4 mm) thick wood respectively. The completed dispenser can be seen in Fig. 118.

Refer to the drawings on these pages for the full plan of the matchbox holder—you should draw out the various parts onto the wood and then cut them out. Start with the back, which is 10 1/2 x 4 1/2 x 3/16 in. (267 x 114 x 5 mm); cut this out and then mark it up in squares as shown in the diagram—this will help you draw the design onto it properly. For the container itself you'll need two sides which are both 8 3/8 x 1 1/2 in. (213 x 38 mm), and a front section which measures 8 3/8 x 2 3/4 in. (213 x 70 mm). You'll need to cut an oblong hole in the front 3/4 in. (19 mm) deep and 5/16 in. (9 mm) in from the sides, and you should make sure you can actually fit a box of matches through the gap.

Fig. 118.
The finished dispenser provides a neat and practical home for your boxes of matches.

Then, cut out the two supports to the size shown in the diagram.

Next, cut out the base. This should be 3 1/4 x 2 5/8 in. (92 x 67 mm) and you'll notice that it has a rectangular notch cut out of the front part, as shown in the diagram. You can now glue the front, sides and bottom together to form the front part of the dispenser.

When it's dry, hold the front against the shaped back—see the dotted lines in the diagram for the exact position. Mark the middle point along the sides in pencil and then put the front to one side. Drill screw holes through the back on the marks and then glue the front and back together. Secure with two screws before the glue has dried. Then glue on the two supports underneath the dispenser (these are mainly for show so don't need to be nailed or screwed on).

Now it's on to the drawer, which is made from two pieces: the floor which is 2 1/4 x 1 1/2 in. (57 x 38 mm) and a front piece which is 2 1/8 x 3/4 in. (54 x 19 mm). Glue the two parts together at right angles to make the main structure. When this is dry, test it to see how it slides in and out of the main frame. If it's fitted correctly, you should be able to retrieve your box of matches

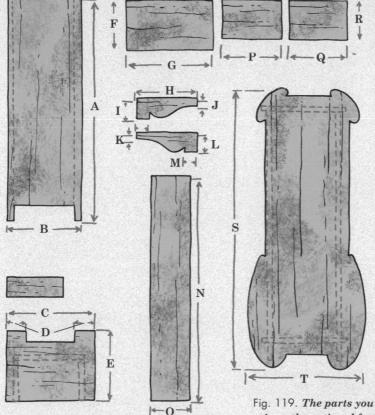

A = $8^3/8$ in. (86 mm)
B = $2^3/4$ in. (70 mm)
C = $3^1/4$ in. (82.5 mm)
D = $3/4$ in. (19 mm)
E = $2^5/8$ in. (66 mm)
F = $1^7/8$ in. (46 mm)
G = $3^1/4$ in. (82.5 mm)
H = $2^5/16$ in. (58 mm)
I = $3/4$ in. (19 mm)
J = $1/4$ in. (6 mm)
K = $1/4$ in. (6 mm)
L = $3/4$ in. (19 mm)
M = $1/2$ in. (12.7 mm)
N = $8^3/8$ in. (86 mm)
O = $1^1/2$ in. (38 mm)
P = $2^1/4$ in. (57 mm)
Q = $2^1/4$ in. (57 mm)
R = $1^1/2$ in. (38 mm)
S = $10^1/2$ in. (267 mm)
T = $4^1/2$ in. (114 mm)

Fig. 119. *The parts you need for the box, minus the optional fretwork overlay.*

without having to pull the drawer completely out of the frame.

After that, you should make the lid, which is actually two pieces of wood glued together to form an inner and outer lid. The outer lid is $3^1/4$ x $1^7/8$ in. (83 x 23 mm), while the inner piece is $2^1/4$ x $1^1/2$ in. (57 x 38 mm). Before you glue them together, make sure the inner lid fits snugly on the top of the dispenser, then fix the inner and outer lids with glue, making sure that they're flush at the back so that they sit neatly against the back of the dispenser.

If you like, you can decorate the front of the dispenser with some fretwork overlay, as shown in Fig. 118. Here the best bet is to come up with a design and then trace it directly onto the wood, so that when you come to cut out the necessary shapes you can follow the lines of the design exactly. Remember to sand the back of the overlay to get rid of any sharp edges caused by the saw, and then glue it to the front of the dispenser.

You can finish the matchbox dispenser with varnish if you like, or leave it in its natural state. Drill a couple of screw holes at the top corners as shown in Fig. 118, hang it on the wall, then load it with matches and you're done.

75 WOODTURNING LATHE

A traditional full-size lathe is a pretty fearsome thing, but this smaller version—which is suitable for turning wood—is actually rather easy to make and can be attached to a table or bench. It also comes apart so you can stow it away.

Fig. 122 shows the main components: a couple of uprights, a bottom bar, a tool rest, and a cord and pedal for driving the lathe. The exact measurements may depend on the amount of space you've got and the kind of jobs you want to do, but as a rule of thumb make sure that the diameter of the wood you want to turn isn't bigger than the diameter of the uprights. So, make sure that the wood you use for the upright is no smaller than 2 in. (50 mm) square and no larger than 3 in. (76 mm) square.

Cut the long upright to 5 ft. 6 in. (1,676 mm) and the smaller one to 3 ft. 6 in. (965 mm). Next, measure up 31 in. (787 mm) from the bottom of the uprights and drive a 3 in. (76 mm) screw into each one; the screws should stick out by 1 in. (25 mm). When the lathe is set up, these will point inwards and actually secure the wood that you want to turn.

The bottom bar needs to be 40 x 3¹/2 x 1 in. (1,016 x 89 x 25 mm) and has a slot running down two-thirds of its length.

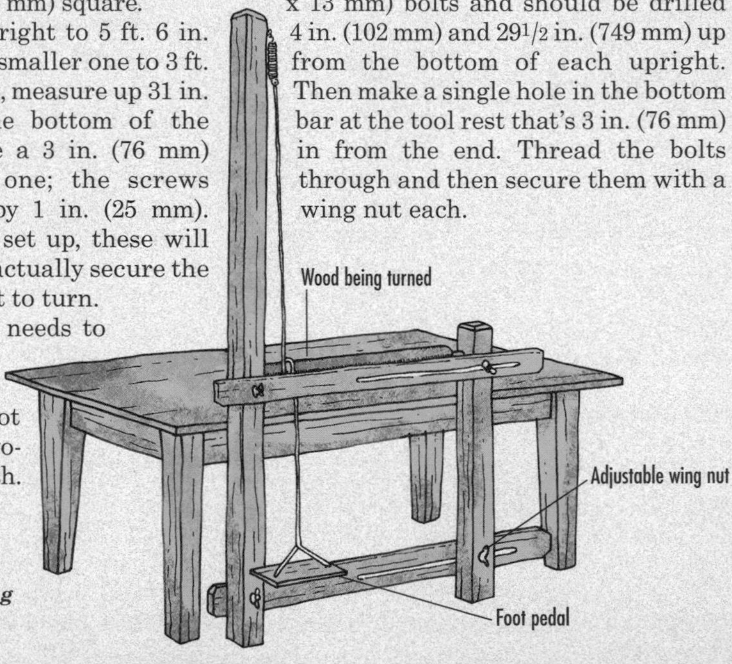

Fig. 120. *The lathe can be attached to your workbench using strong G clamps.*

The slot should be 10 in. (254 mm) from one end, and 5 in. (127 mm) from the other, and ¹/2 in. (13 mm) deep. To make the slot, drill out a series of ¹/4 in. (13 mm) holes and then knock out the bits in between with a chisel and clean up with a saw and sandpaper. Make the tool rest (the upper crosspiece) and slot in the same way, but ensure that it's only 3 in. (76 mm) wide.

Next, bevel off the top edge of the tool rest ⁵/8 in. (16 mm) each way and then saw ³/4 in. (19 mm) off the bottom corners of the tool rest and all four corners of the bottom bar. Finish with a chisel and sandpaper.

Now drill the holes that will allow you to attach the bottom bar and tool rest to the pair of uprights. The holes need to take 4¹/2 to 5 x ¹/2 in. (114 to 127 x 13 mm) bolts and should be drilled 4 in. (102 mm) and 29¹/2 in. (749 mm) up from the bottom of each upright. Then make a single hole in the bottom bar at the tool rest that's 3 in. (76 mm) in from the end. Thread the bolts through and then secure them with a wing nut each.

Wood being turned

Adjustable wing nut

Foot pedal

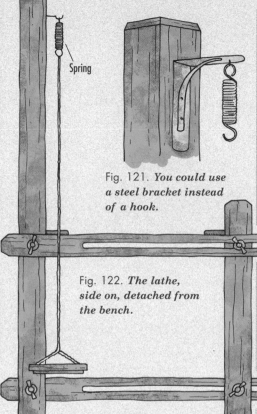

Fig. 121. *You could use a steel bracket instead of a hook.*

Fig. 122. *The lathe, side on, detached from the bench.*

by fixing a strong screw hook into the inner side of the long upright, about 4 in. (101 mm) down from the top. Next, slip a 6 in. (152 mm) steel spring onto the hook and then tie a length of cord onto the other end of the spring. The cord should be long enough to reach the floor—probably about 72 in. (1,829 mm) in all. Leather cord is the best for this because of all the friction involved in driving the lathe, but if you can't get leather of that length, try and make a cord yourself that has a leather section in the middle.

The foot pedal is a piece of wood $8^{1}/_{2}$ x 5 x 1 in. (216 x 127 x 25 mm), with two holes drilled into it about 6 in. (152 mm) apart to take the end of the cord.

Using the lathe takes a little practice but works like this: the wood you're working on is held at either end by the two 3 in. (76 mm) screws that you took the ends off, while the wing nuts allow you to adjust the working length of the lathe. When the wood for turning is in place, you wrap the cord

Remember the two screws you secured on the inner sides of the uprights? It's time to file the heads off and round the ends to make a sort of cone shape. After that, attach a couple of G clamps to the backs of the uprights so that you can secure your lathe to a bench or table. The exact position of these will vary depending on the height of the bench, but the underside of the top clamp arm should be level with the top of whatever surface you're using.

You're going to drive the lathe with some good old-fashioned pedal power, which will require a hook, spring, cord and somewhere to put your foot. Start

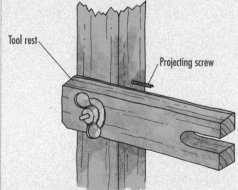

Fig. 123. *The beveled tool rest is attached to the upright using a wing nut. This end is fixed while the other end slides to accommodate different lengths of wood.*

around it once and then attach it to the hook at the bottom of the spring. Working the foot pedal then pulls the cord, which turns the wood; the spring ensures that the pedal comes back into the resting position after every push of your foot.

To work with a piece of wood you'll need to bore a small hole in either end— $1/4$ in. across and $1/4$ in. deep (6 mm x 6 mm)—so that it can be "gripped" by the two screws. Operating a lathe like this is worth a book in itself, but you can count on it being frustrating at first and later both rewarding and productive, allowing you to shape wood in ways that would be otherwise impossible.

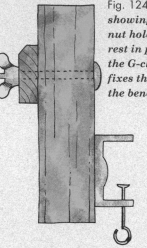

Fig. 124. *Side view showing the wing nut holding the tool rest in place, and the G-clamp that fixes the lathe to the bench.*

Shed Shorts

- Why is the U.S. Drug Enforcement Agency hoping to add a shed to its national museum in north Virginia? Because it had been turned into a sophisticated indoor laboratory for growing hallucinogenic mushrooms that produced thousands of dollars-worth of funky fungi every week.

- Residents in a small Scottish town thought that nobody loved them until 17,500 undelivered letters, packets and parcels were discovered in a local postman's garden shed.

- San Antonio, California—jurors sat stunned as the contents of a local man's shed were paraded in court. Rather than forks and spades, officers discovered 51 assault rifles, shotguns and pistols, including an AK-47 and a particularly unpleasant Mossburg 12-gauge with a pistol grip.

- In Kentucky, a 65-year-old woman in dispute with a local company has been sleeping in her shed for two years.

- In sleepy Wiltshire, 30 years of neighborly love went up in smoke when one claimed that a two-room, 9 ft. tall concrete building was a shed, while the other said it couldn't be because it had patio doors.

- James Dyson, the vacuum cleaner mogul, used his shed to develop prototypes for his revolutionary bagless cleaner.

- In Scotland, the shed of a retired merchant banker and hapless golfer became home to more than 3,000 golf clubs and stacks of how-to books and instructional videos. Despite spending an estimated £50,000 he still played with a 19 handicap.

SHED LIFE

76 A GARDEN BASKET

This is a neat flat wooden basket of the kind used by gardeners. It's easy to make and looks good too.

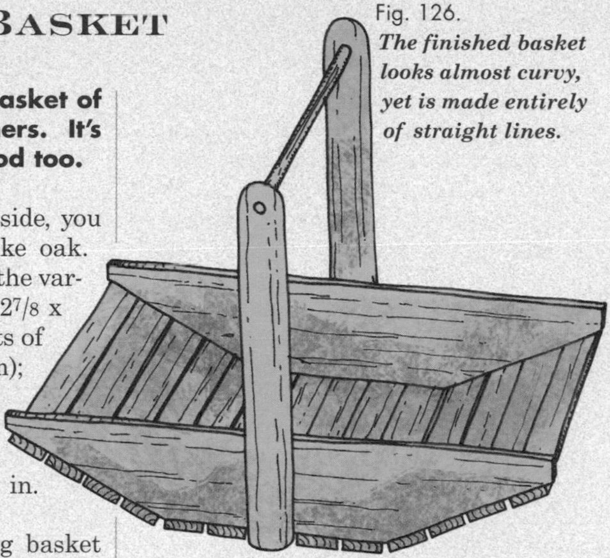

A s the basket is for use outside, you should use a hardwood like oak. Here are the measurements for the various bits. Two sides of $18^{1}/_2$ x $2^{7}/_8$ x $^{5}/_8$ in. (470 x 75 x 15 mm); 13 slats of 10 x $1^{1}/_4$ x $^{5}/_{16}$ in. (254 x 32 x 9 mm); one handle of $1^{5}/_8$ in. (270 mm) dowel, $^{7}/_{16}$ in. (12 mm) in diameter; and two supports for the handle of $11^{3}/_8$ x $1^{5}/_8$ x $^{5}/_8$ in. (290 x 40 x 15 mm).

Draw the distinctive sloping basket shape on the two sides and cut them out. If you have the tools or the know-how, you can try and "slope" them, but it's much easier to keep them straight. Oddly enough, although the finished basket is all straight lines, it actually looks quite curvy. To make sure the two sides' dimensions are as identical as possible, put one on top of the other, line them up and make any necessary adjustments. Bore $^{1}/_8$ in. (4 mm) "pilot" holes at each end of every slat, then turn the sides upside down and fix the first slat across one end of the flat part of the bottom. Use brass screws for this.

Aim to get five slats across the bottom of the basket and a further four up each side; use a small piece of wood as a divider if you're concerned about not getting the gaps between them even enough; and don't make them too big.

Bore partway into the tops of the handle pieces and glue the dowel rod between them. Then line up the two vertical pieces to make sure they're at 90 degrees to the basket and, from the inside, fix them to the sides with brass screws.

Fig. 126. *The finished basket looks almost curvy, yet is made entirely of straight lines.*

Fig. 125. *If you can't gauge the spaces between the bottom boards by eye, use a narrow piece of wood as a spacer to ensure that all the gaps are even.*

77 CLAY MODELING

A traditional craft that still thrives today—car manufacturers regularly use it to make models of new proto-types—clay is one of the most versatile materials around. It comes in many varieties and colors and various different brands, and finished models are usually either air-dried or baked in the oven.

Beginners should start with some-thing small, partly because it takes less time to get results and partly because larger models require what's called an "armature" or wire frame, designed to support the model while it's being constructed—take a look at the rabbit's ears on this page and you'll see what we mean. A water bowl for the cat or dog may not be very glamorous, but it's also a forgiving project that allows for a few rough-and-ready edges. Alternatively, a sign for the shed is a good place to start—though jewelry for a girlfriend may be more politic—and you can make excellent scenery for model railroads out of clay.

Although you can buy specialty modeling tools like rollers and cutting wheels, almost any-thing will do to start with— an old lollipop stick, the wooden end of a paint-brush or an opened paper clip are all useful makeshift tools. A little-plant spray bot-tle filled with water will help to keep your model malleable,

and if you have to leave it overnight cover loosely with a moist plastic bag, sealed round the edges.

Most modelling clay needs to be "warmed up" before you can work with it—knead it like bread—and if you have to put it aside for any reason, an air-tight container will keep it workable. If you're using clay that air-dries, cover it with a wet cloth while you're leaving it out to dry, as this will help prevent cracks forming.

(By the way, if you want to make a really inexpensive start in modeling, you can make your own "clay." All you need is one cup of salt, a cup of flour and half a cup of water. It's easy to mold and can be baked in the oven at about 250°F or 120°C.)

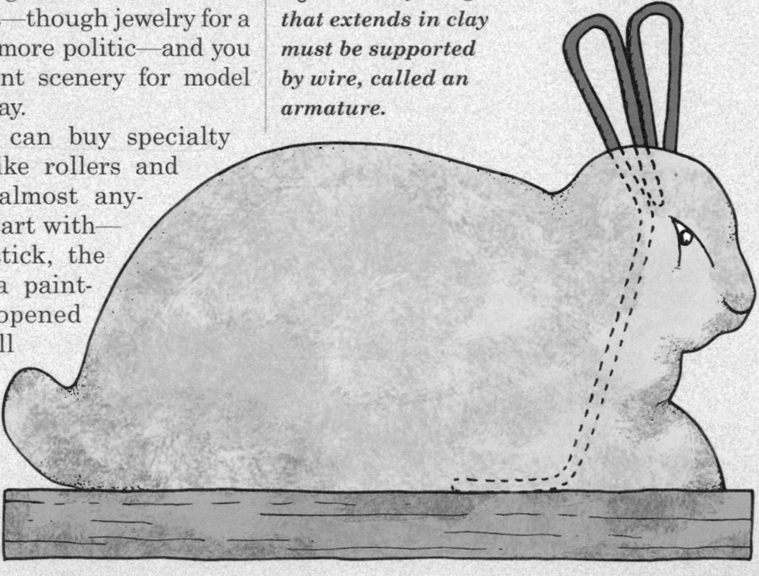

Fig. 127. *Anything that extends in clay must be supported by wire, called an armature.*

(78) SPIDER PUPPET

Because of the number of "wires" involved (actually, it's cotton thread) and the way the legs are jointed, this spider will walk across the floor so realistically that it'll give arachnophobes a real scare.

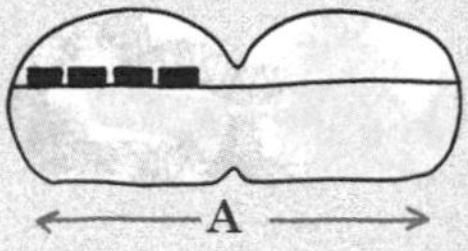

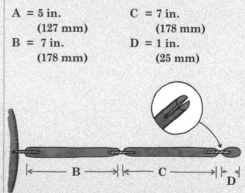

Fig. 128. *The body is made of two pieces of softwood.*

You'll need a bit of softwood for the body, 5 x 2¼ x 1 in. (127mm x 57 x 25 mm) and shaped with a chisel and sandpaper as shown in Fig. 128. Next, take a small saw and cut the head—but only the head—of the spider in half lengthwise, then make another cut at right angles where the head joins the body and lift off the top half of the head.

You'll need 16 7 x ½ in. (178 x 13 mm) dowel rods for the legs. To make a leg, cut a horizontal notch into the end of two of the dowels and then glue a tiny piece of leather into each notch so it acts like a hinge. You'll also have to make an angled cut into the dowels below this joint so that the leg can bend naturally—see Fig. 129. Make another notch at the foot end, and glue another

piece of leather there; then add a blob of putty to make the foot. Make a last notch at the other end of the leg and glue in a slightly longer piece of leather. Repeat until you've made all the legs.

Glue the leather tabs at the end of the legs onto the front part of the spider and then glue the half-head piece you cut off back on top to secure them. When the glue's dried, you can paint the spider.

The control bar is simply three pieces of wood nailed into an "H" shape—the two long sides should be 18 in. (457 mm) long and the crosspiece 9 in. (229 mm) long. Add four screw eyes down each of the long sides for the legs and then one fore and aft of the crosspiece for the body. Finally, use black cotton string and small nails to attach the controller to the spider.

A = 5 in. (127 mm)   C = 7 in. (178 mm)

B = 7 in. (178 mm)   D = 1 in. (25 mm)

Fig. 129. *A side view of a leg, including segment measurements and hinges.*

(79) TOOL CABINET

If you leave your hand tools lying around, pretty soon they're going to let you down. Instead, why not give them a neat little home with this handy cabinet?

You can make this tool cabinet using just pine and batten. Here's the "recipe"—remember, if you buy it ready planed, you'll save a lot of time. Two sides of 33 x 8 x $5/8$ in. (838 x 203 x 166 mm); one top of 26 x 9 x $3/4$ in. (660 x 229 x 19 mm); one top shelf of $23^3/8$ x 4 x $1/2$ in. (594 x 102 x 13 mm); one middle shelf of $23^3/8$ x 2 x $1/2$ in. (594 x 51 x 13 mm); one bottom shelf of $23^3/8$ x 5 x $1/2$ in. (594 x 127 x 13 mm); one cabinet bottom of $23^3/8$ x $7^1/4$ x $1/2$ in. (594 x 184 x 13 mm); four door edges of $30^1/8$ x $1^1/2$ x $3/4$ in. (766 x 38 x 19 mm); four door rails of $11^3/8$ x $1^1/2$ x $3/4$ in. (289 x 38 x 19 mm); two three-ply door panels of $29^5/8$ x $8^7/8$ x $1/8$ in. (753 x 225 x 4 mm); and one three ply back piece of 33 x 24 x $1/8$ in. (838 x 610 x 4 mm).

Mark out the shelf grooves on the cupboard sides as shown and gouge them out to $5/16$ in. (9 mm) deep working from the back. Cut across the grain with a big chisel and remove most of the waste before sawing to the right depth and sanding to finish off. You'll have to cut a notch at either end of the bottom one so that it sits flush to the front of the cabinet; then test the shelves by fitting them into both sides. Next, put on the top and mark the position of the sides, then cut two stopped grooves to take the top of each side. Make any adjustments necessary to square the cabinet.

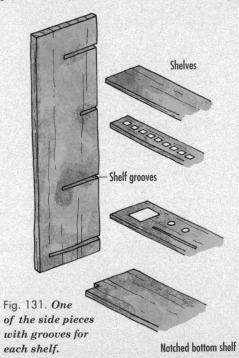

Fig. 130. *Keep all your tools in their special place with this cabinet.*

Shelves

Shelf grooves

Fig. 131. *One of the side pieces with grooves for each shelf.*

Notched bottom shelf

Before you glue the cabinet together, you need to make the holes in the bottom and middle shelves. The ones in the middle shelf are 5/16 in. (9 mm) square and 1 in. (25 mm) apart. Mark out both sides, bore through with a 5/16 in. (9 mm) drill and then chisel out the square shape—first on one side and then on the other. The bottom shelf is more complicated but it can be prepared in the same way. Note that the holes for the two largest chisels have little slots in them. With the larger slots, start by boring a hole at each end and then chiseling out the rest. Although the holes here are for the selection of tools shown in the drawing, you can easily adapt the shelves to suit whatever you want to store, and drill holes accordingly.

With the shelves done, shape the bottom edges of the two sides, plane a 1/2 in. (13 mm) bevel around the top and then glue and nail the whole thing together. When you attach the back, nail or screw it to the shelves as well as the sides and bottom edge.

Fig. 133 shows the mortise-and-tenon joints you'll need to make for the door frames. The doors themselves should fit so that they sit neatly on the sides and can be closed properly. Use two hinges, top and bottom, for this; for neatness, recess them by the depth of the hinge.

The position of the clips on the door will depend on what tools you want to hang there, but fortunately their shape and dimensions will work for nearly everything. There are two kinds. First, you'll need a 5/8 in. (16 mm) square block. Take another piece of wood 2 1/2 x 5/8 x 5/16 in. (63.5 x 16 x 9 mm) and shape

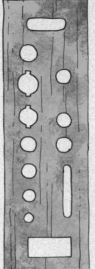

Fig. 132. *The exact holes you drill in this shelf will depend on the tools you want to store.*

the corners, then screw it into the other block—not tightly, because you need it to turn, like a handle. Then glue the block to the door and secure it with screws from the other side. The other clip is a fixed piece of wood 3 x 3/4 x 5/8 in. (76 x 19 x 16 mm). Cut a chunk out of this by sawing down 5/16 in. (9 mm) on the shortest side and 1 1/2 in. (38 mm) in from the end—secure this so that the side with the missing chunk is facing the door. Fit a little turn button on the front of the doors to keep it closed when you're not using it, and then stain and varnish to finish.

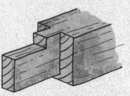

Fig. 133. *Mortise-and-tenon joints like this are strong and will keep the cabinet nice and rigid.*

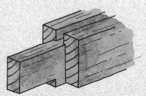

(80) ELASTIC-DRIVEN MOTORBOAT

The easiest way to make one of these is to cannibalize an old existing boat or something you've picked up in a second-hand shop. If you can't find anything suitable, you'll have to carve it yourself from a block of wood by hollowing out the hull with a chisel or gouge (you can make it easier to scrape out by using a red-hot poker to char the wood in the center).

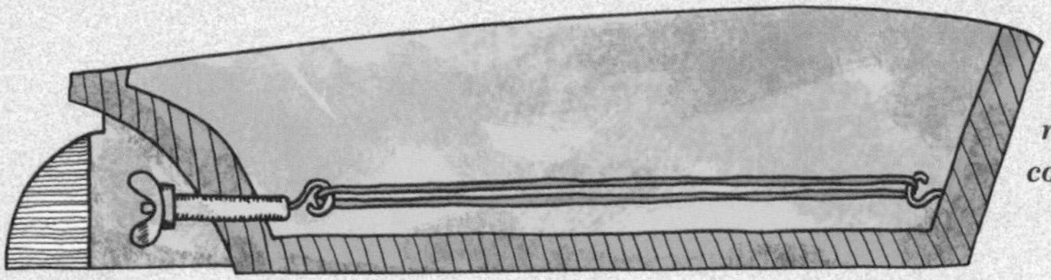

bow; then slip a little bit of cycle-valve tubing over both hooks to stop them cutting into the elastic.

Attach four strands of strong elastic to the hook—and the shaft and your boat are ready for action! You should be able to get as many as 100 turns on a set-up like this, which will fairly hurl your boat across the water. One more thing: to extend the life of your elastic, use your fingers to lubricate it from time to time with liquid soap.

Fig. 134. *The elastic band motor and rudder fitted to the completed hull.*

Y ou could buy a ready-made propeller from a model shop, but if you want to do it yourself you can carve it from a single block of hardwood. It should be about half the depth of the hull (not including the keel, if it has one). You can make the shaft from a bicycle spoke—cut a section about 1 3/4 in. (45 mm) long from the end of the spoke that's got a thread on it. Bend the end without the thread to make a small hook.

Next, drill a hole through the stern to fit a 1 in. (25 mm) section of 1/8 in. (3 mm) brass or copper tubing. Grease the little propeller shaft, push it into the tube, and then pack both ends of the tube with cotton odds and ends to make sure it's waterproof. Put a washer on the end of the shaft that's sticking out, screw in the propeller and tighten it with a small nut. Get a small screw-eye hook and turn it into position at the

The Celestial Shed

A shed epitomizes practical, down-to-earth pursuits like gardening and DIY. However, shed owners are increasingly opening their eyes to other, further-reaching possibilities—and they don't come much further-reaching than building your own shed-observatory. The principle is simple: you need a sturdy plinth for the telescope, a shed big enough for the telescope and you, and a roof that slides off when you're stargazing. Make the roof separately, stick casters down the sides, build runners into the top of the shed sides and add a frame next to the shed to roll the roof onto. When it's rolled back, lock it in place with strong hasp clasps.

81 PAPER PUZZLE

You don't necessarily need anything complicated to make your own fun and have your friends scratching their heads. Just some paper, paint, scissors and a couple of books will do the trick.

The first is a deceptively simple paper puzzle. Take a square piece of paper or card and, with a pencil, mark the halfway point along the top edge and along the left side. Next, take a ruler and join these two dots together with a straight line. Then draw a line from the first dot down to the bottom right-hand corner and then another line from that corner back up to the second mark (the one halfway down the left-hand side of the paper). You've now got a square of paper with a triangle marked out on it. Cut along the lines and you'll end up with four different-sized triangles. Scramble these on your desk and get a friend to put them back together again so they form a perfect square. It'll take them longer than you—or they—think!

82 MATCHSTICK PUZZLES

Fox your friends with these tricks. All you need is a box of matches.

First, take a match and bend it in the middle (don't actually break it) to form a "V" shape. Place it on the top of an opened, empty bottle and then put a coin on top—the coin needs to be small enough to fall into the bottle. Then ask a friend to "drop" the coin into the bottle without touching it or the bottle, the match or the table.

The solution? Let a drop of water fall onto the angle of the match where it's bent and wait a moment. The moisture will cause the match to open slowly and the coin will drop into the bottle. (No, lighting the match doesn't count!)

Or, how about trying this one? Take 12 matches and arrange them into a large square made up of four smaller squares. How can you turn these four squares into three by removing and repositioning only four of the matches? Simple. Take away the two matches that make the top-right corner. Then take away the two that make the left-hand corner. You're left with two squares arranged in a diagonal shape. Use the four matches you've removed to make a third square on the same angle as the others.

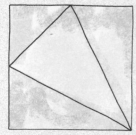

Fig. 135.
It looks simple, but solving this puzzle is harder than you think.

Fig. 136. *Matches are great for simple, shape-based tricks.*

83 MAKE YOUR OWN PAPER

This is a great way to recycle your used printer/photocopier paper and at the same time create some unique stationery of your own. It's simple but messy, and unless you're fortunate to have electricity in your shed you'll need to negotiate with whoever runs the kitchen in your house—and make sure you clean up afterwards.

You'll need about 50 sheets of used white paper, 10 sheets of matte-colored paper (from a magazine or old wrapping paper) a couple of 7 x 5 in. (177 x 127 mm) old picture frames, a plastic screen larger all round than your picture frames, a staple gun (hammer and tin tacks will do), a blender (hence the need for negotiating some kitchen time), disposable kitchen cloths, a sponge and a big washing-up bowl (which should be wider and deeper than the picture frames), some newspaper, a packet of gelatin, and anything you want to use to pep up your paper—such as dried flowers, potpourri, dried herbs and so on.

Get your plastic and stretch it tight over the front of one of the empty picture frames, then staple or tack it down firmly to the back on all sides.

To prepare, start with your used printer/photocopy paper. Rip it into 1 in. (25 mm) square pieces and soak them all night in a bucket of water; do the same with your colored paper, but soak that separately. You'll need about four times as much plain white paper as you will colored paper.

The next day, grab a good handful of the wet white paper and pop it into a standard-sized household blender (not one of the little personal ones), then add hand-warm water until it's about three-quarters full. Blend it together until it's the consistency of porridge. Then empty it into the washing-up bowl and repeat with three more loads.

Get in there and give the pulp a good stir with your hands. It's should be really sloppy at this stage—about 90 percent water—so if you need to add more warm water, don't be shy. After you've done that, dissolve the gelatin in hot water and then stir it into the

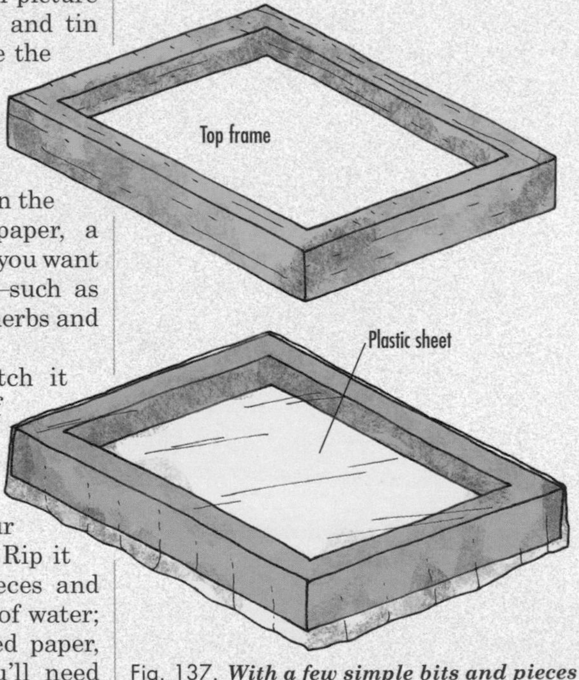

Top frame

Plastic sheet

Fig. 137. *With a few simple bits and pieces you can recycle old paper to make new, personalized stationery.*

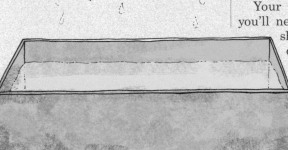

Hold the frame steady

Fig. 138. *It's important that you hold the frame over the bowl until all of the excess water has dripped back into it.*

tightly together. You dip them vertically into the washing up bowl, then bring them out and hold them horizontally so that the pulp covers the screen.

It's important not to let too much pulp cover the screen—otherwise your paper will be super-thick. Hold it there for a couple of minutes so that all the excess water can drip back into the bowl. As the paper is sitting there, you can sprinkle a bit of dried this or that into a corner as a visual "accent."

Your paper needs to dry flat, so you'll need plenty of space. For each sheet, prepare a couple of sheets of newspaper with a kitchen cloth on top. Lift off the top frame and then turn the other frame over on top of the cloth, pulp side down. Gently pat the back of the plastic with the sponge to soak up any water that's left—but don't actually wipe it—and make sure you get into all the corners. Keep patting the back until your newly minted paper starts to separate from the plastic. Peel it off carefully onto the kitchen cloth. Then go and do another sheet.

Your paper should dry in a night. Gently peel away the kitchen cloth (if it turns out to be damp on the other side, flip the paper and leave it to dry again). When you've got a stack of paper (!) put some heavy books on it for a day or two—the pressure will help to keep the paper flat.

By the way, don't throw away excess pulp—instead, drain the water and dump the rest in your worm hotel (page 88). Worms just love damp paper, and it's very satisfying to recycle something that's already been recycled!

pulp—this will stop ink from running on your paper and ruining the results.

Blend in some of the soaked colored paper and any other bits and pieces you want to form your paper. Don't go mad, especially with the dried flowers and other stuff—in fact, you may want to add just a bit of this directly onto the paper later on. Blend in the extra bits for about 15 seconds or so.

Now you need to dip the two frames into the pulp. The frame with the plastic sheet stapled to it should be on the bottom, with the sheet facing down; the other frame should be on top so that you can hold the backs of the two frames

84 BLACK-CAT BIRD SCARER

There are few things more effective for keeping the birds away from your vegetable garden than a cat, but, if you don't fancy actually owning one, you can still fool our feathered friends into thinking that you've got one on guard.

The simplest bird scarer is a full-on cat mask. Draw out the shape on a piece of outdoor plywood and then paint it black. When it's dry, use either little bits of mirror or crystals for the eyes and glue them on. Punch a hole at the top and attach some string. As it spins in the wind, the eyes will flash and frighten the birds away.

Even more effective—draw a cat shape in silhouette with the tail curling out and upwards on a piece of thin sheet metal. It doesn't need legs—just make two sharp points with which to stick it in the ground. Cut out the shape with a hacksaw and finish it with a metal file. Paint the whole thing with metallic black and then glue on a couple of little mirror fragments for the eyes.

Fig. 139. *Simple but effective, the mirrored eyes reflect the sun and scare away birds.*

85 FISHING ROD

A fishing rod can bring you hours of pleasure—and making this version couldn't be simpler.

All you need is a length of straight bamboo cane, about 6 ft. (1828 mm) long, and some eyed screws. Leave a gap of about 18 in. (457 mm) at one end and then screw in the first eye. Repeat with the others at intervals of about 6 in. (152 mm). The last ring should be as close to the other end of the rod as possible. You can pick up a cheap fixed-spool reel at a yard sale and bind it on to the rod with gaffer tape in front and behind.

If you don't want to use a reel at all you can attach the line directly to the rod. Don't use any rings at all. Instead, make a small hole about 1 in. (25 mm) from the end of the rod—you'll have to do this very carefully so that the cane doesn't split. Get a strong piece of elastic about 12 in. (305 mm) long, with enough give so that it pulls to 18 in. (457 mm) when fully extended. Thread the elastic through the hole and knot it securely. Wrap a bit of tape either side of the hole to help stop the cane from splitting, then tie the other end to a length of fishing line. The elastic will allow you to play the fish you hook more easily.

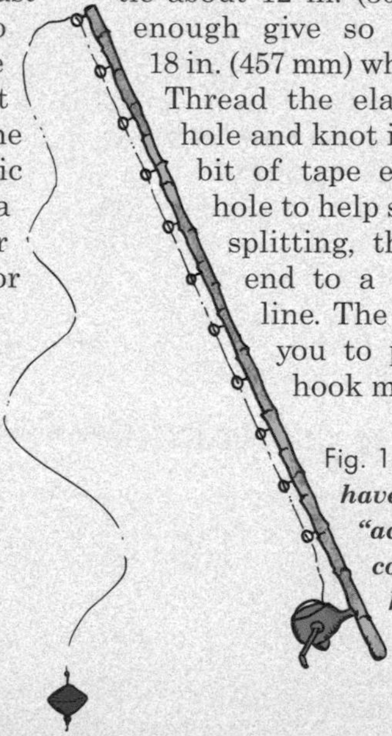

Fig. 140. *It may not have much of an "action," but used correctly it will help you catch plenty of fish.*

86 SHOVE HA'PENNY BOARD

This classic pub game is harder to play than it looks—fortunately, though, it's straightforward to make and looks good, too.

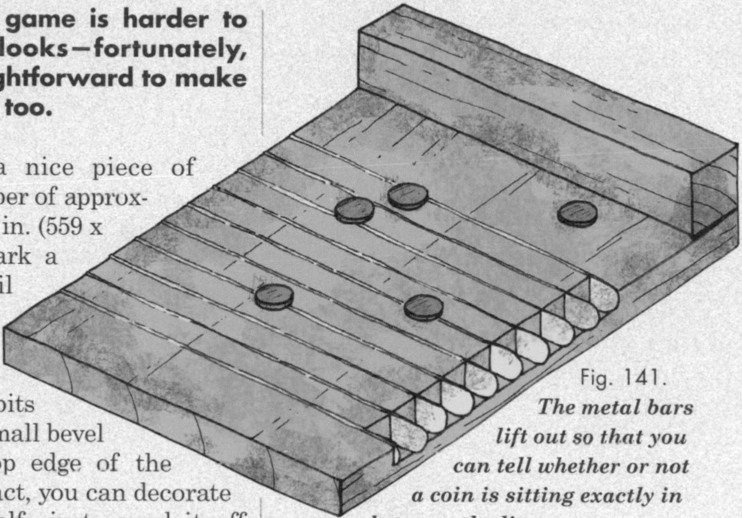

Get yourself a nice piece of reclaimed timber of approximately 22 x 10 x 1 in. (559 x 254 x 25 mm). Mark a line with a pencil 2 in. (51 mm) in from the end and saw it off. Plane and clean up both bits of wood. Make a small bevel all around the top edge of the smaller piece (in fact, you can decorate this to suit yourself—just round it off with sandpaper if you like) and then gouge out a shallow indent about 5 in. (127 mm) long in the middle of the top and sand it smooth. This is to take the chalk needed to score the game. Next, bore two holes through the small piece of wood at either end and then screw it in place on top of the large piece.

Measure in about 3 in. (76 mm) from the other end of the board and draw a line across it. Next, take the coin you're intending to play with and place it so that it's a fraction behind the line; add a fraction on the other side of the coin and that's where your next line goes. Continue drawing out lines across the board until you've got ten. At the end you should have a series of lanes running across the board, wide enough so that a perfect "shove" will result in the coin fitting between them with a tiny bit to spare on either side. If you like, you can now simply saw across each of these lines just enough to score the surface of

Fig. 141.
The metal bars lift out so that you can tell whether or not a coin is sitting exactly in between the lines.

the wood, then sand the grooves with a bit of fine sandpaper. To finish, stain the wood if it needs it, and varnish.

If you want to be a bit more sophisticated (and to sort out any "it-was-in"/"oh-no-it-wasn't" arguments) you'll need to get hold of some thin metal rods, preferably brass. Depending on what you can get hold of, saw down into each of the lines so it's exactly the width and depth of the rod. Then, fit each rod into its slot, making sure that they all fit flush and that the surface of the board is even. Now, if there's a dispute about a coin being in or out, you just lift out one of the rods—if the rod moves the coin, it doesn't count.

87 A LAND YACHT

A variation on the traditional go-kart, this adds a sail that will propel the yacht around any large flat area like a beach or a common.

Cannibalize whatever you can from other sources. Wooden packing cases are good for making the base (vehicles like this aren't prized for their looks, after all) and old buggy wheels still on their axles are a great start; you can even use the wheels off an old bike—just take the tires off first and get a sheet-metal shop or hardware store to fit axles to them. If you must buy wood, then batten and pine will do fine. You'll also need rope, some 1½ x 2 in. (38 x 51 mm) wire nails, three bolts, 8 ft. (2 m) of bamboo of about 1½ to 2 in. (38–50 mm) diameter to make the mast, and two 6 ft. (1.83 m) of ½ in. (13 mm) diameter bamboo for the sail. Then you want some plain calico to make a square sail 6 ft. (1.83 m) high/wide; get someone to sew the top and bottom edges for you, and slip the thinner lengths of bamboo into them.

Fig. 142 shows the measurements for the frame. You'll need two pieces of 6 ft x 2 in x 2 in. (1.83 m x 51 mm x 51 mm)

and two more of 18 x 2 x 2 in. (457 x 51 x 51 mm) for the four sides. These should be nailed together at the corners and then covered, fore and aft, by two pieces of beveled 2 in. (51 mm) batten to conceal the joins.

Saw up four 2 ft. (609 mm) lengths of batten and nail them on as shown in Fig. 142 to make a seat. Sit on it and work out where your feet are likely to be, then hammer on another batten for a footrest, about halfway between the seat and the front axle. Add two more battens, front and back, to further secure the frame.

The front and back axles should be about 6 in. (152 mm) from each end. The front axle needs three holes bored in it—one in the center for the bolt which attaches it to the frame, and two at either end to take the length of knotted rope, so you can steer. The bolt also

A = 15 in. (381 mm)
B = 2 in. (51 mm) battens
C = 6 in. (152 mm)
D = 24 in. (610 mm)
E = 18 in. (457 mm)
F = 6 in. (152 mm)
G = 3 in. (76 mm)
H = 6 ft. (1829 mm)
I = 14 in. (356 mm)

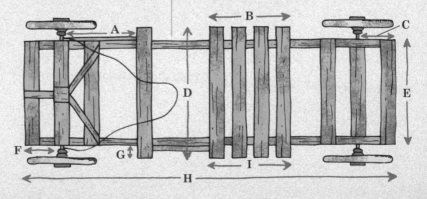

Fig. 142.
The land yacht with everything in place except the mast and sail.

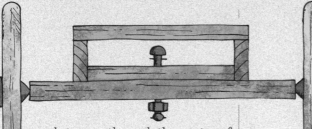

Fig. 143.
The completed front-wheel section. The bamboo mast slots into the top piece of wood.

needs to pass through the center of a little batten frame, arranged as in Fig. 143. The back axle has two holes bored in it, and is then bolted onto a batten crosspiece as shown in Fig. 142. Once that's done, the frame is complete.

Make up two blocks of wood 2 in. (51 mm) square. Drill a hole about 1/2 in. (13 mm) wide into one block, drilling down about 1/2 in. (13 mm), and then nail it to the crosspiece over the front axle. The little "socket" you've just made should be pointing upwards. Drill a hole the same width—but all the way through—in the second block and push the bamboo mast through it. (This fit is tricky: it needs to be tight enough to secure the mast, but you also need to be able to remove the mast to transport the yacht.) Locate the end of the mast in the socket of the first block and then position the second block about 2 ft. (609 mm) above that. Measure off and then nail three pieces of batten obliquely to the upper block (see Fig. 144) and then to the crosspieces, as shown in Fig. 142.

Fit a small plug of wood with a screw eye into the top of the mast—this is for the rope to run through so you can raise the sail. Thread the rope through the eye and tie one end to the middle of the bamboo pole at the top of the sail— you'll need to make a hole in the calico for this, but remember to stitch round it to prevent tearing. Both ends of the bamboo pole at the bottom of the sail should have the same wooden plug-and-screw-eye arrangement as the top. The screw eye at the mast end of the bottom pole attaches to a little hook screwed into the upper square wood block. With practice, you'll be able to control the sail by tightening and slackening the rope.

One last tip: to brake, either drop the sail or turn the yacht into the wind.

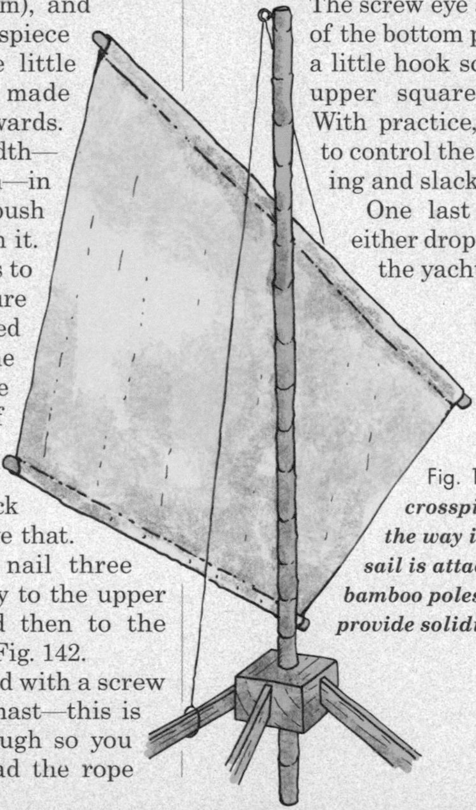

Fig. 144. *The mast crosspiece showing the way in which the sail is attached to the bamboo poles. Three stays provide solidity.*

88 MODEL SAND MOTOR

The sand motor works just like a water wheel, and although it's not going to run your house lights, the model shown here can generate around 1/10 horsepower at 200 revolutions per minute. Given that the hopper can carry about 90lbs of sand, you should be able to run it for an hour without having to refill. That's pretty good.

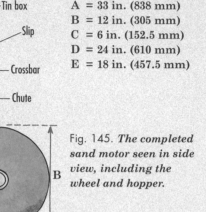

A = 33 in. (838 mm)
B = 12 in. (305 mm)
C = 6 in. (152.5 mm)
D = 24 in. (610 mm)
E = 18 in. (457.5 mm)

Fig. 145. *The completed sand motor seen in side view, including the wheel and hopper.*

All the necessary sizes are marked on the diagrams, but if you want to make a smaller—or bigger!—version, just adjust the measurements in proportion. Use a square biscuit tin to make the hopper, cut the lid in half and then solder the remaining half to the box. The width of the tin will dictate how wide your base is and how far apart your sides are.

In this example, the base is made from a piece of wood 24 in. (610 mm) long and about 1½ in. (38 mm) thick; the two uprights are 33 in. (838 mm) long, 9 in. (228 mm) wide and 1 in. (25 mm) thick. Use five long screws per side, from the bottom of the base up through the two sides, to secure them. Remember: depending on the size of the tin, you may have to adjust accordingly. Cut a V shape at the top of each side (see Fig. 146 for the correct angle) and then cut, glue and screw two other pieces of wood across the V so as to support the hopper; they should be about 4 in. (100

mm) deep and 1 in. (25 mm) thick. You'll need about 1 in. (25 mm) underneath the front support to leave room for the chute.

There's going to be a lot of sand up there, so secure the tower with a cross brace of 1 x ¼ in. (25 x 6 mm) pine. As you look at the tower face on, run one brace from top left to middle right and the second brace from middle right to bottom left. Angle the ends, then glue and nail them securely.

To make the wheel, cut out two circles of three-ply plywood, about 3/16 in. (5 mm) thick and exactly 12 in. (305 mm) in diameter. Next, mark the exact center of each disc and then draw a smaller circle on them of exactly 10 in. (254 mm) in diameter. Drill a ¼ in. (6 mm) hole through the center of each.

The wheel needs eight spokes, or "vanes," which are made of wood 2 x 1¼ x 3/16 in. (51 x 32 x 5 mm). These need to be glued around the center hole, equal distances apart—see the diagram for the precise arrangement, and note that they don't radiate out like wheel spokes but are inclined outwards. Once the glue has set, tap in two nails per vane from the outside of the wheel to finish the job.

Next, take eight other pieces of wood of the same dimensions and glue them into the gaps between the vanes, around the circumference of the 10 in. (254 mm) circle. You may need to adjust the length of these slightly, depending on how accurately you were able to position the original vanes. When you're done, give every join a light coat of glue to make sure they're sealed—otherwise the sand is going to trickle through and impair the effectiveness of the motor. Glue a square block of wood at the center and then glue and nail the second disc on top like a sandwich. Drill into the center block from each side so the holes meet, and then poke through a 12 in. (305 mm) silver steel tube, 1/4 in. (6 mm) in diameter.

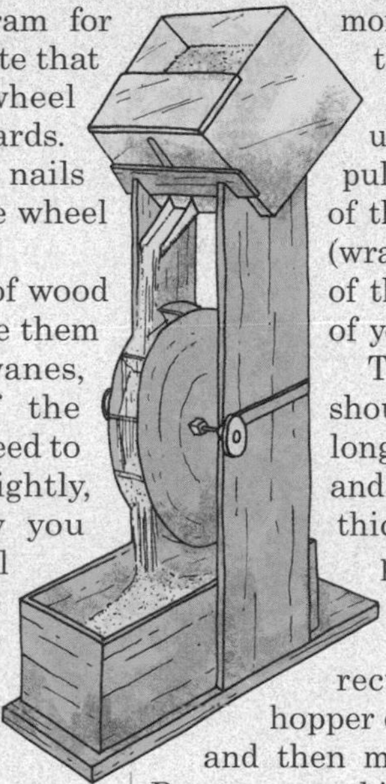

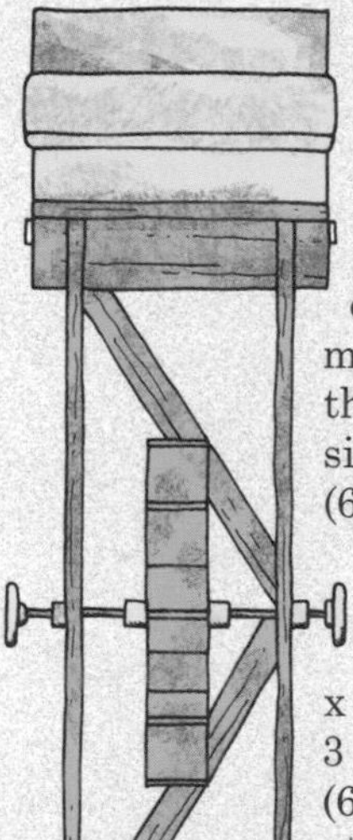

For the metal axle supports you'll need two flat brass plates 8 x 3/4 x 1/8 in. (203 x 19 x 3 mm). Drill a 1/4 in. (6 mm) hole for the axle at the end of each one, and then make three more holes in each to take the screws that will secure them to the uprights. Fix a small pulley wheel at either end of the axle to keep it steady (wrap a drive belt round one of these to power the model of your choice).

The bottom container should be 18 in. (457 mm) long, 6 in. (152 mm) high and made from 1/2 in. (12 mm) thick wood, screwed into position from the under the base. Finally, cut a 1 1/4 x 1 in. (32 x 25 mm) rectangular hole in the hopper directly above the wheel and then make a U-shaped chute. Put some sand in the hopper, adjust the chute until it's in the correct position and then solder it to the tin. Screw a small bracket into the tin above the chute and then make a "door" out of wood or metal, the width of the chute, with a narrower "handle" that slips up and under the bracket. You can then pull the handle up to open the chute and push it down to close it.

Fig. 146. *The motor can generate around one-tenth of a horse power.*

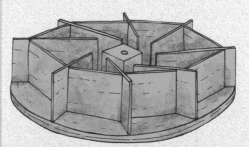

Fig. 147. *The inside of the wheel—the walls must be attached firmly and be "sandproof" or the motor will lose power.*

89 CARD BOX AND TRUMP INDICATOR

This elegant box can be used both to store your playing cards and also indicate to other players which suit is being used in those games which feature trumps.

It can be made entirely of fretwood. For the base, you'll need a piece of wood 4³/4 x 3³/4 x ³/16 in. (121 x 95 x 5 mm) and for the lid another of 4¹/2 x 3¹/2 x ³/16 in. (114 x 89 x 5 mm). Round the edges of both the lid and the base with a file and sandpaper. The long sides of the box should measure 4 x ¹³/16 x ³/16 in. (102 x 21 x 5 mm) and the short sides 3 x ¹³/16 x ³/16 in. (76 x 21 x 5 mm). There's not going to be any strain on this box, so you can chamfer the ends of the four sides to a 45-degree angle and then—having made sure they fit nicely—just glue them together.

Fig. 148.
The open card box, with the trump indicator being used in a game.

When the glue's set, glue the bottom onto the four sides and then secure permanently with small screws, which you can drive up through the bottom of the box.

The lid has a thin layer of fretwood on the top for decoration and another inside the lid for the actual trump indicator. The lid overlay should be 3³/4 x 2³/4 x ¹/16 in. (95 x 70 x 2 mm) while the inside layer is 3¹/4 x 2 x ¹/16 in. (83 x 51 x 2 mm). Use a fretsaw to cut the four suits into the lid overlay—one in each corner. You can then run a slot that's ¹/8 in. (4 mm) wide between the corners, about ¹/4 in. (13 mm) in from each edge. If you don't fancy your skill with a fretsaw

enough to produce decent copies of the four suits, then you may be able to buy metal stick-on ones at a hobby or craft shop that will do almost as well. Have a crack at those slots though.

Now let's move on to the underside of the lid. You'll see from the illustration that you need to mark two arcs on the fretwood, through which the trump indicator swings. The smaller arc has a radius of 1¹/2 in. (38 mm) and 2¹/8 in. (55 mm). The arrow indicator meanwhile should be cut into the shape shown here, and measures 1⁵/8 x ⁵/16 in. (36.5 x 8mm); pin it to the underside of the lid with a fretnail. Make sure it's secure enough so that it won't fall off, but loose enough so that you can swing it

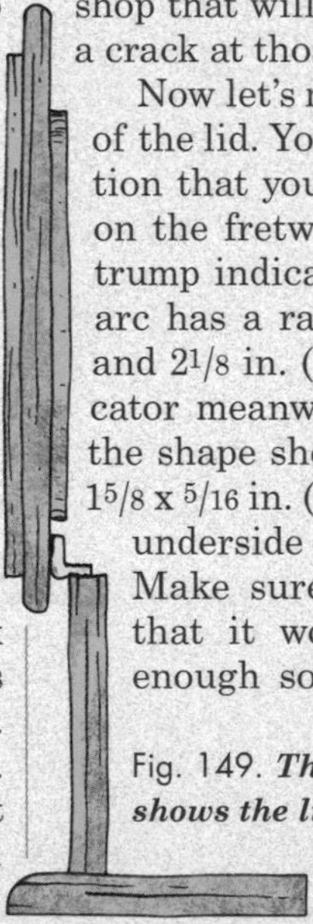

Fig. 149. *This side view of the box shows the lid and hinge in their correct positions relative to each other.*

around the arc to point to the correct trump. Again, you can either draw and then cut out the four trump signs using a fretsaw or buy stick-on ones. If you do, you may have to move them slightly further up the lid than shown here so that the indicator can still move freely.

Glue both the overlay and the underside to the lid and let them both dry. You'll then need two 5/8 in. (16 mm) long hinges screwed into the top edge of one of the long sides—the other half of the hinge is screwed into the underside of the lid, 3/8 in. (11 mm) in from the edge. That way, when you open the lid, it rests neatly against the side. If you find the lid doesn't stand as well as you'd like, chamfer away a little of the back edge of the box so that, when opened, the lid tilts back slightly more than 90 degrees.

For a final touch, you can use some green baize (like you'd find on a snooker table) or felt to line the inside bottom of the box. This will keep your cards in good condition.

A = 2³/₄ in. (70 mm)
B = 3³/₅ in. (95 mm)

Fig. 150. *The finished lid overlay with each card suit cut out neatly.*

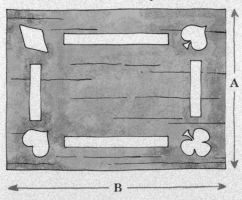

90 CARTESIAN DIVER

This fascinating little experiment shows the effect of gravity and buoyancy on an object in the water. All you need is a plastic bottle (one that you can squeeze) full of water with a lid, some Plasticine, a cup and a plastic pen top.

Fill the cup with water. Take the pen top and press some Plasticine around the edge of the hole. The idea is to get enough Plasticine on the pen top so that it floats vertically in the water with the hole (and Plasticine) under water and the top sticking up clear of the water, like the tip of a fishing float. You'll need to experiment to get the amount of Plasticine just right—that's what the cup's for.

Fill the bottle with water and put the "diver" into the bottle so that if floats the way it did in the cup. Screw the lid onto the bottle. If the diver sinks, unscrew the top, remove it and take off a little of the Plasticine; then try again. With the top back on, squeeze the bottle and you'll see the diver sink—stop squeezing and it will rise to the top again. As you squeeze you compress the air trapped in the pen top, which decreases buoyancy; when you release the bottle, buoyancy is restored.

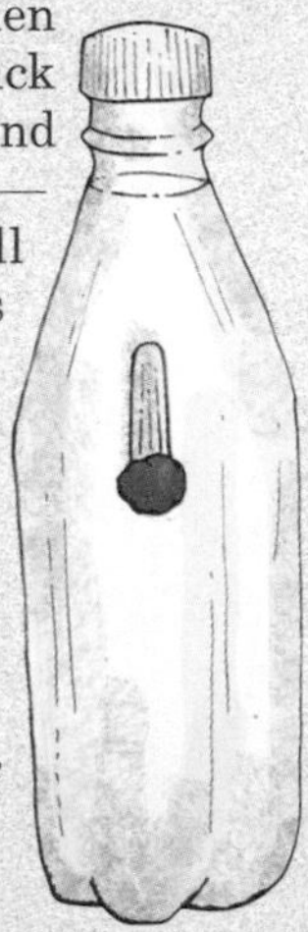

Fig. 151. *Squeeze and release the bottle to see your "diver" rise and sink.*

91) TOBOGGAN

Although there are many different kinds of toboggan you can make, this is one of simplest and most effective—it's especially good if you're fortunate enough to get deep snow. All you need is some pine, nails and screws, and two strips of sheet iron to "shoe" the runners.

While the pine should be 1 in. (25 mm) thick throughout to give it strength, the exact length and depth will depend on the size of the person riding it. Start by sawing of the angles on one side piece—the runner—as shown in Fig. 152. Obviously, both angles should face the same direction. Then round off the edges at the front of the runner. Next, measure in about 2 in. (51 mm) from the back of one runner and saw down 1 in. (25 mm); measure a further 2 in. (51 mm) along the runner from this cut and then make another one. Saw out the wood in between until you've got a notch that's 1 in. (25 mm) deep and 2 in. (51 mm) across. Make another notch exactly the same size near the front of the runner. Next, lay the first runner on top of the second one and use that as a guide to mark out the position of the angled saw cuts front and back, as well as the two notches. Cut out the second runner so that it's the same as the first.

Now you need two strips of pine about 2 x 1 in. (51 x 25 mm) and long enough to take the width of a passenger's bottom—about 15 in. (381 mm) should be OK. Fit these crosspieces into the slots and position the toboggan so that the two runners are about 12 in. (305 mm) apart. Screw the crosspieces into the slots on the runners so that they're flush at one end but the other end is sticking out by about 3 in. (76 mm). Then saw off the protruding bits of wood. Now you need to cut another piece of wood to the size of the top of the sled and nail it to the runners.

For a faster, smoother ride, add two narrow strips of sheet metal to the bottom of each runner. Get an ironmonger to prepare these for you with about four screw holes in each—and make sure that there's a hole 1/2 in. (13 mm) from either end to help keep the metal flush with the runners.

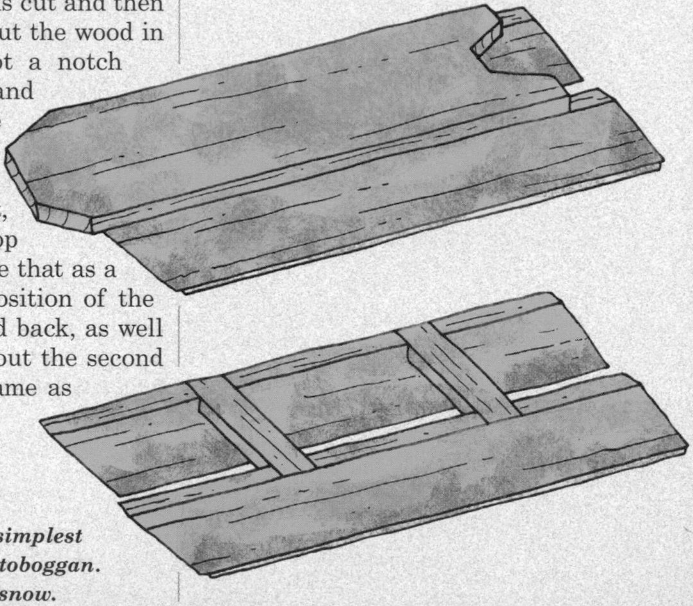

Fig. 152. *This is one of the simplest and sturdiest designs for a toboggan. It's especially good in deep snow.*

⁹²WEATHER VANE

This is a simple device designed to sit on top of a shed or other building and show you which direction the wind is blowing.

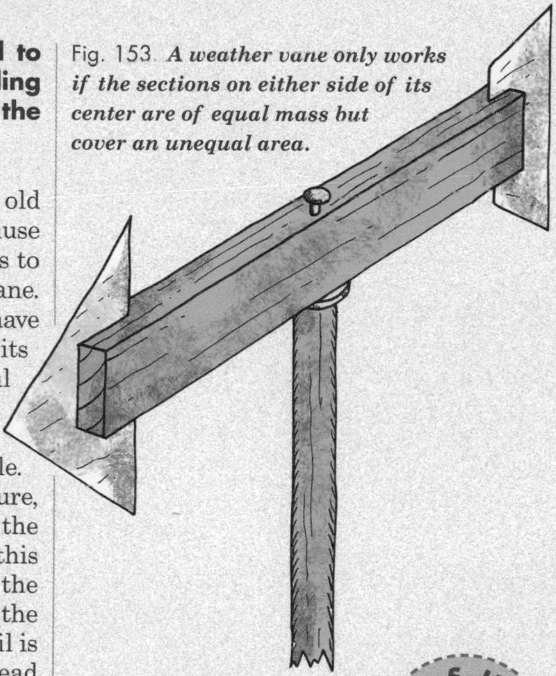

Fig. 153. *A weather vane only works if the sections on either side of its center are of equal mass but cover an unequal area.*

Y ou can't just throw together any old design and expect it to work because there are a couple of important rules to remember when making a weather vane. First, the ornament at the top must have an unequal area on either side of its center; second, it must have an equal mass on either side of its center. That's because it's essentially a vertical plane on top of a vertical axle. When the wind blows it exerts pressure, and because the area of one side of the vane—if it's a cockerel, for example, this would be the tail—is larger than the other, the wind exerts more force on the tail than the head. The result? The tail is pushed away from the wind and the head points towards the wind.

With the physics lesson over and done with, we can now make a simple weather vane like this. Cut two slits, 1/2 in. (13 mm) deep at either end of a 12 in. (305 mm) piece of wood. Halfway along, hammer a long nail all the way through the wood; spin the wood round it until it turns easily. Cut the arrow and the tail from an old bit of sheet metal and glue them into the slots front and back.

Any stout stick will do for the vertical pole, but an old broomstick handle's the right size. Hold a washer on top of the broomstick and then bang the nail into it. This will help the weather vane to move more freely. Place your weather vane as high as you can safely secure it.

The Literary Shed

As every shed enthusiast is aware, nothing surpasses the peace and quiet of a shed; and it is equally well known that writers are generally fond of solitude. This may be why so many authors are to be found tapping away at the bottom of the garden—though "sheds" could be stretching the definition, given some of the palatial examples they work in. Shed fans in the writing world include Philip *(His Dark Materials)* Pullman, Louis *(Captain Corelli)* de Bernières and the great Daphne *(My Cousin Rachel)* du Maurier.

● S H E D ●
L I F E

93 THE NAIL PUZZLE

A good puzzle should be easy to create and hard to solve—and this nail puzzle fits the bill perfectly. To make it you'll need two nails between 3 and 4 in. (76 and 102 mm) long, plus a pair of pliers. If you've got a vice, it'll make the job easier.

Fig. 154. *The seemingly impossible nail puzzle—with practice you'll be able to detach them in seconds.*

Bend the two nails into the shape shown in the diagram. The key to creating a good—and difficult-to-solve—nail puzzle is to get them as identical as you can and to make sure the gap between the two bits of bent nail is too narrow for the other nail to get through.

Once the nails are bent, push the point of each one through the loop of the other (see Fig. 154) and then twist and slide them together. As you do, the two loops will slide one inside the other and the nails will become attached via the loops. Give it to a friend and they'll find it all but impossible to get the nails apart, because there doesn't seem to be a gap anywhere in the puzzle that's wide enough.

Here's the solution:
Take the head of each nail between your thumb and first finger and bring the point of the left-hand nail over the point of the right one; this will bring the head of the right nail over the head of the left nail. Keeping the nails crossed, ease the two spaces together with a gentle slide and then twist them slightly towards each other. Get it right and, as if by magic, the puzzle will come apart in your hands.

It's not easy to do, and you might find that it takes some practice, but after a while you'll be able to do it quite quickly. If you conceal the exact hand movements in some way, this will prolong the mystery and keep your friends fooled for longer.

The Lady Shed

"Man" sheds tend to be messy, although many suffer an occasional burst of prettification when the lady of the house briefly descends to smarten the place up. (Fortunately, it only takes a few weeks of neglect to return the shed to its original state.) "Lady" sheds are a more personal and permanent statement, and can be anything from bijou personal cinemas to meditation rooms, to home offices and even tiny spas. Given that a recent survey in the UK concluded that a properly kitted-out shed could add as much as five percent to the value of a house, it's obviously a trend to be encouraged . . .

SHED LIFE

94 CATAPULT

Time was when a boy's pocket only carried the essentials of life—a few coins, some string, an inky handkerchief, a boiled sweet, some blotting paper... and one of these.

Although you can buy catapults in the shops—they're very popular with anglers—it's more fun to make your own in the traditional way; and there are still those who believe that the best catapults are created by nature and that all you have to do is find them. That means spending some time looking for the perfect piece of wood.

What you're after is a good, strong hand-sized fork to cut from a tree. Cut it about 6 in. (154 mm) below the fork and leave about 6 in. (154 mm) for the two arms. To test for weaknesses, tie your elastic on any old how and flex it 20 or 30 times. If it feels solid, it's a keeper.

You can strip the bark from the branch if you like, but usually it's best to wear the catapult in before you get too fancy. Use a sharp knife to make a groove around the diameter of each arm near the top to act as a guide for your elastic. The knots on page 19 will help you to tie on the elastic/rubber.

You can buy elastic, but rubber cut from an old tire inner tube is great for catapults, and you can use leather to make the holding pocket—the tongue of an old shoe works well. You can punch holes at either end of the pocket to take the elastic and then reinforce them with a pair of press-in eyelets. Alternatively, poke a series of holes lengthways across the middle of the pocket and thread the elastic in and out of them before attaching it to the arms.

A catapult is a toy, but a dangerous one. Never point it in the direction of other people, even if you're mucking about, and never fire anything at an animal or a bird. Don't use a catapult anywhere where there are lots of windows and never fire anything straight up in the air. In other words: have fun, but use it responsibly.

Fig. 155. *You'll be able to knock over plenty of empty tin cans with one of these—just make sure that there's no one in the line of fire.*

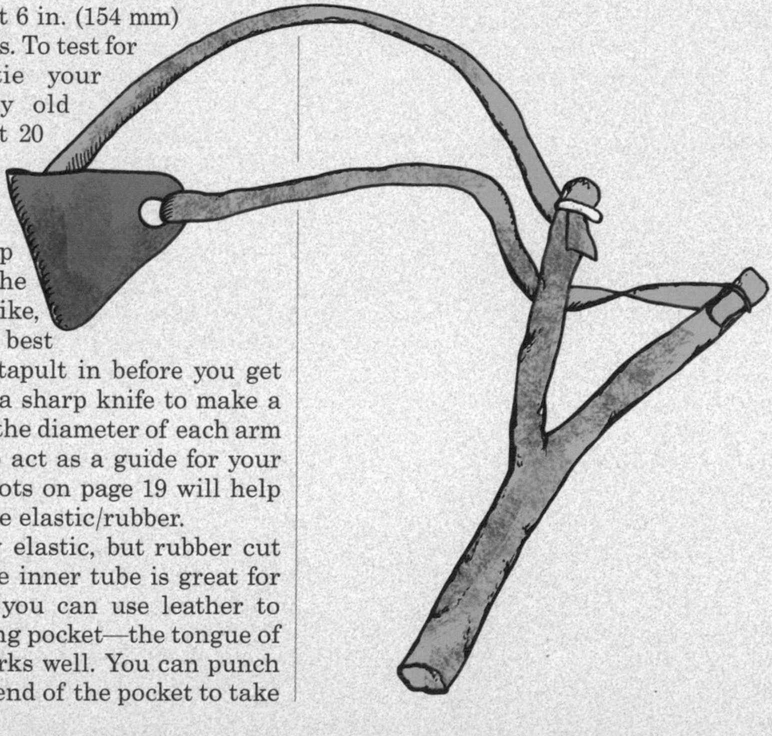

95 MAGNETIC TRICKS AND EXPERIMENTS

Magnets are great fun and can be used in all sorts of entertaining ways. For example, if you've got a much younger brother or sister that you don't mind taking advantage of, you can fox them by putting a toy car on a piece of paper and then holding a flat magnet underneath it. You'll then be able to move the car around the paper using the magnet—but without touching the car. This is a real head-scratcher for the under fives.

There's a more interesting variation on this which involves holding a flat bar magnet under the paper and pouring iron filings (which you can get from toy and hobby shops) onto the surface—the filings will be distributed in a pattern along the lines of magnetic force.

Or how about this? You'll need half a dozen round magnets with a hole in each. Take a pencil and a blob of putty. Stick the pencil in the putty and then drop the first

magnet over the pencil. Gently lower the next magnet over the pencil until you can feel it push against the first one; if it doesn't, remove the second magnet, flip it over—to reverse the polarity—and try again. When you've got all six on the pencil, they'll just hover there. Spooky.

Next, try the dancing magnet. You'll need four flat magnets arranged as the corners of a square—exactly how close together you can put them will depend on how strong they are. Then tie some string to a fifth magnet and hold it over the other four. The magnetic field generated by the four flat magnets will cause the other one to "dance" above them. When your magnet's moving freely, glue the other four into position.

Finally, try this. Take a paper clip and straighten it out. Rub the south end of a magnet down the lower half of the paper clip about 50 times. Then turn the paper clip over and rub the north end of the magnet down the lower half the same number of times. This will turn the straightened paper clip into a magnet, and you'll be able to use it to pick up other clips. (Try cutting it in half— you'll find that you've just got two smaller magnets.)

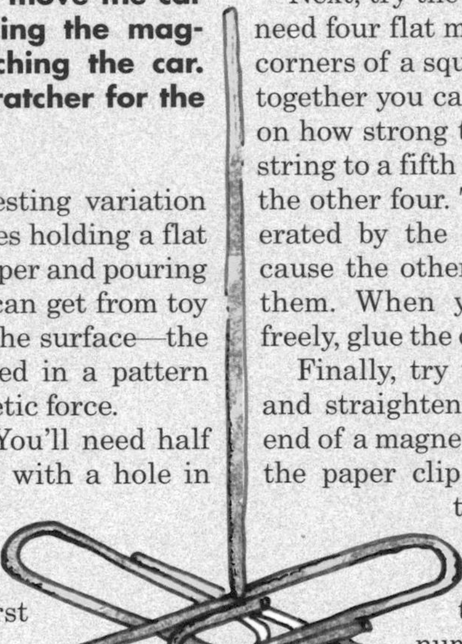

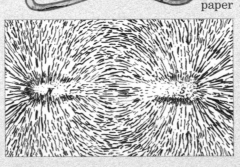

Fig. 156. **You can even use a magnet to make other magnets—such as this straightened paper clip, for example.**

Fig. 157. **Iron filings make great patterns when manipulated with a magnet.**

96 BIRD BOX

There are many different bird boxes you can build, but many of these are overly elaborate and can actually scare the birds off! Not so this design, which is perfect for smaller birds like blue tits and sparrows.

You'll need one piece of exterior plywood measuring 25³/4 x 5⁷/8 x ³/8 in. (655 x 150 x 12 mm); and a second piece measuring 24¹/2 x 5¹/2 x ³/8 in. (625 x 140 x 12 mm).

Fig. 158 shows how to mark and then cut out the ply to the correct shapes. The wider, 5⁷/8 in. (150 mm) wood is for the roof and sides (which slope), and the narrower 5¹/2 in. (140 mm) piece is for the front, back and bottom of the bird box. The sloping, overhanging roof is important because it forces rain to run away from both the entrance and the main part of the box, thus helping to keep the occupants dry. Once you've cut the pieces out, make a hole in the front of the box—this should be no larger than 1¹/4 in. (32 mm), which is plenty big enough for a sparrow; the bottom of the hole should be about 5¹/8 in. (130 mm) from the bottom of the box.

Nail the box together and then drill four small holes into each hanger. Screw the hangers into the back—the screw heads should be inside the box—and then use the other holes to attach the box to a tree. If you're feeling fancy, you can adjust the top of the box and add a hinge; otherwise, glue a strip of Velcro to the top edge of each side and equivalent strips to the roof. Now you can easily lift off the roof when you need to clean the box.

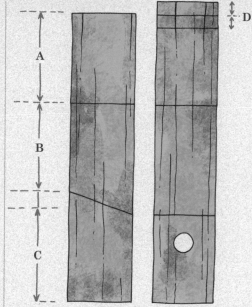

Fig. 158. *The wood for the bird box complete with measurements. The door should be at least 1 in. (25 mm) in diameter.*

A = 8 in. (205 mm)
B = 7³/4 in. (200 mm)
C = 9³/4 in. (250 mm)
D = Strips to be used for the hangers

Fig. 159. *The roof is removable, which makes access easier and allows you to keep the bird box clean.*

97 DESK ORGANIZER

This handy desk tidy will give you somewhere to keep all your bits and pieces. It's got an open-drawer design—though you could add simple drawers if you want. It's made of ordinary pine.

Take three pieces of pine cut to 16 x 9¼ x ½ in. (406 x 235 x 13 mm) to make the end and vertical middle piece of the organizer. You can leave them as they are, but it's more interesting if you give them a curved edge at the top. Simply draw this out on one of them, cut it and then use this as a template for the other two. Sand the curves smooth, then take one of the boards and saw ½ in. (13 mm) off the shorter side—you have to do this because the middle divider rests on the bottom board and thus needs to be slightly shorter than the two end pieces.

*Fig. 160. **This desk organizer will help you keep the clutter in a home office under control.***

You now need to cut shelf slots into the middle divider and one of the end pieces—each slot is ½ in. (13 mm) wide and ⅛ in. (3.5 mm) deep. Measuring up from the bottom of the side piece, the slots should be placed at 3 in. (76 mm) 6¼ in. (159 mm), 9⅜ in. (239 mm) and 12⅜ in. (315 mm); remember that the divider is ½ in. (13 mm) shorter, so each shelf position will be lower by exactly that amount. When you've done, flip the divider over and make another slot 2½ in (63.5 mm). up from the bottom on the other side—this will take the long shelf (which you haven't cut or fitted yet).

Cut out four shelves, each measuring 9¾ x 6 x ½ in. (248 x 152 x 13 mm), and glue them into the slots. You've now got a lopsided set of five shelves. Put them aside to dry.

Next, cut a piece of wood 13 x 9¾ x ½ in. (330 x 248 x 13 mm) and make two slots, front to back, that are ½ in. (13 mm) wide and ⅛ in. (3.5 mm); you can actually space these however you like, but think in terms of what you're going to store between them—magazines perhaps?—before you decide. Cut out two partitions to fit into the slots. Again, you can shape the tops if you like; it's up to you. The dimensions for these are 9¾ x 9 x ½ in. (248 x 229 x 13 mm). Glue them into place and leave to dry.

Take the other side piece and measure up 3 in. (76 mm) from the bottom make a slot for the shelf that's ½ in. (13 mm) wide and ⅛ in. (3.5 mm) deep. Finally, prepare a piece of pine 19 x 9¼ x ½ in. (483 x 235 x 13 mm) for the base.

Now you can assemble the desk organizer. Start by gluing and nailing the "lopsided" shelf piece you first built to the base, as shown in the diagram. Next, glue the other side in place and, before it's dried, slot in the long shelf with the two vertical dividers on it. Once this is in the correct position you can completely secure the second side with glue and then nails. You should now have the entire organizer apart from the back. Set it aside to dry.

Finally, you need a piece of hardboard measuring 19 x 16 in. (483 x 406 mm). Lay the hardboard down, then put the organizer on top of it. The bottom and sides should match perfectly, but you'll need to mark where the tops of the various dividers fall on the back board. Then join these up using a ruler. You can now cut out the shape you've just drawn along the top of the back board. When you've finished, nail it to the back of the organizer and use sandpaper to clear off any rough edges.

The Go-Faster Shed

Mark Reynard fulfilled a boyhood dream when he built a 1300 cc racing car in his shed. It went from 0 to 100 mph in seven seconds and had a top speed of 160 mph; but he made one small miscalculation—he couldn't get it out of the shed. Instead, he had to remove the roof and all the walls and then watch as a crane picked up the car and lifted it over the top of his house and down into the street. His first race should be interesting—the only practice he's ever had is on a computer.

98 MUMMIFIED FISH

This is a completely bizarre "experiment" that is also great fun and only needs a fish, a plastic box (slightly larger all round than the fish) and some baking soda (also known as sodium bicarbonate).

Dress the fish (i.e., scale and gut it, but leave the head on). If you don't like this, you can buy one already dressed—like a trout or mackerel—from a fishmonger's. Fill the plastic box to about 2 in. (51 mm) deep with the baking soda. Next, fill the stomach cavity with baking soda. Put the fish in the container and then cover it with even more baking soda until it's encased by about 2 in. (51 mm) all around.

Leave the fish for a week and then remove it from the box. Clean out all the baking soda and then repack it with fresh stuff. Leave it for another week. When you take the fish out the second time it will have turned leathery—mummified, if you will—because the baking soda leeches out all the moisture in the fish. Don't eat it.

99 AN ANCIENT DOCUMENT

This is a bit of fun which you can use to produce a fake antique document or certificate, complete with an authentic-looking wax seal.

Get a sheet of 8½ x 11 in. paper and prepare the document. If your handwriting is up to the job, then that's great, but if it isn't then you can cheat by using a script font on your home computer—most PCs will include at least one font that looks like handwriting.

Once the document's done, you need to stain it. Tea is as good as anything—although some people swear by coffee and vanilla, this has a strong aroma—so boil some water and then put a couple of bags into a cup. Pour in the boiling water and allow it to stand for about 15 minutes. Next, you can either take the tea bags out—carefully—and rub them all over the paper, or empty the tea into a shallow metal tea tray and then dip the paper in it, a bit like developing a photograph. Then leave it to dry.

Next, you'll need a short piece of string and the top off a jar—the smaller the better (something like a lip-balm jar is perfect). Use a hacksaw to cut a small notch in one side of the lid. Position the lid so this notch is at 12 noon and cut two more notches at five and seven o'clock.

Make two string-sized holes in the bottom of the paper, about ½ in. (13 mm) apart and thread the string through them. Then take both ends of the string and lay them across the top notch in the lid. Then separate the two ends and lay one across the five o'clock notch and the other across the seven o'clock notch. Melt wax into the lid. As you do, it will cover the string, and when it sets you'll be able to cut the circle of wax out of the lid with the string still inside. You can then decorate the seal as you please.

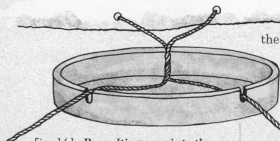

Fig. 161. *By melting wax into the dish, you'll secure the ribbon and produce an authentic-looking seal.*

100 SKATE SCOOTER

To complete this project successfully, you'll either need some metalwork skills of your own or access to a sheet-metal shop or old-fashioned hardware store. If you do, you'll find this quick to make a lots of fun to use, despite the retro styling.

Start with a piece of knot-free (this is important) hardwood that measures 16 x 5 x 1 in. (406 x 127 x 25 mm) and drill four holes as shown in Fig. 162. Each hole is 3 in. (76 mm) in from the end and 1 in. (25 mm) in from the side. You'll then need to cut a slot in the front of the skate to take the single wheel—the exact dimensions of this will depend on the size of the wheels you've managed to find, though of course they should all be the same size. You can cut away the corners if you like—but it's unlikely to improve the aerodynamics!

Get your hardware store to sell you two steel axle rods to fit your wheels—the front axle is 4½ in. (114 mm) and the back is 8 in. (203 mm)—and ask them to drill holes in both. You'll need two in the front one, 1½ in. (38 mm) in from each end, and four for the rear. To work out where these should be placed, take

your wood base with you and line it up with the rear axle so that the two inner holes line up with the holes you drilled in the wood and the two outside holes are positioned properly to take the cotter pins that will hold the wheels on. Four thin bolts will hold the axles securely in place.

A rectangular piece of leather makes a good foot strap, secured under a strip of wood each side that is then screwed into the base. The heel grip is bent and shaped tin and can be secured to the base with screws; do the same with the straps in front of it.

Use thin screws throughout and drill holes for them first—that way you won't split the wood.

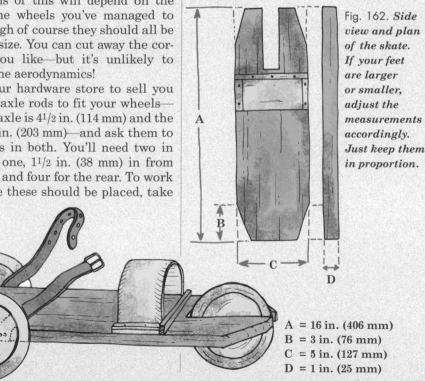

Fig. 162. *Side view and plan of the skate. If your feet are larger or smaller, adjust the measurements accordingly. Just keep them in proportion.*

A = 16 in. (406 mm)
B = 3 in. (76 mm)
C = 5 in. (127 mm)
D = 1 in. (25 mm)

121

101 SECRET BOX

As its name suggests, this is a box with a secret. From the outside—and to the uninitiated—it appears impossible to open, but, as you'll see, the design conceals a cunning inner drawer which can only be opened if you know how.

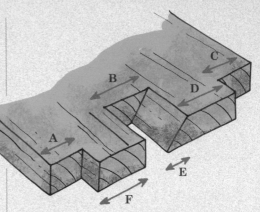

For wood you'll need 24 x 6 x 1/4 in. (610 x 152 x 6 mm) of satin walnut cut—and this is important for the finish—across the grain. You'll also want 8 ft. (2,438 mm) of 5/8 in. (16 mm) beading.

First, cut out the 11 pieces of wood as shown in Fig. 163. Leave a little extra around each edge so that you can smooth them to ensure a tight fit. Start by preparing piece 4 and then finish off 1 and 2 and then glue them to edges of 4 and secure with 3/4 in. (19 mm) panel pins; make sure that the indents at the

A & B = 6 x 3 in. (152 x 76 mm)
C – F = 6 x 2½ in. (152 x 63.5 mm)
G   = 5½ x 2 in. (140 x 51 mm)
H   = 2½ x 2½ in. (63.5 x 63.5 mm)
I   = 2 x 2¼ in. (51 x 57 mm)
J   = 3 x 2¼ in. (76 x 57 mm)
K   = 3 x 3 in. (76 x 76 mm)

Fig. 163. *The block of wood cut into the 11 pieces needed for this project.*

Fig. 164. *The notches shown here will engage the hooks on the drawer in Fig. 165.*

A = 3/8 in. (10 mm)
B = 1/2 in. (13 mm)
C = 3/8 in. (10 mm)
D = 1/2 in. (13 mm)
E = 1/4 in. (6 mm)
F = 1/2 in. (13 mm)

end of 1 and 2 are at the same end. Finish off 3 and then fix and nail it to 1 and 2 to complete the outer box.

Next, prepare piece 8 (including the little cut-outs) and fix it inside the back of the case with glue and pins so that it's flush with the indents at the end of pieces 1 and 2. Now, although we don't need it yet, cut out and prepare piece 10. This is easily the trickiest part of the job, which is why you should have a look at Fig. 164, which shows the angle (45

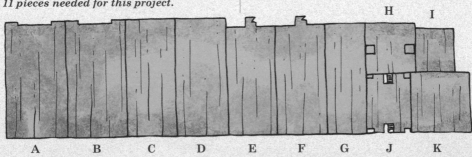

degrees) and the measurements of the catch on each side. Piece 10 fits against piece 8, with the points of the angles upwards and inwards—you have to make sure that the points are level with the bottom edge of the cut-outs on piece 8.

Use piece 7 to make the bottom of the secret drawer and 5 and 6 to make the sides. Before you glue and pin these, check that the "hooks" at the back of each fit properly into the notches on piece 10. Then cut out and prepare piece 10 and secure it between pieces 5 and 6 to form the back of the drawer.

When it's dry, slip the drawer into the outer case and the hooks at the back of pieces 5 and 6 should poke through the cut outs in piece 8. Then, pop piece 10 into position and check that the hooks properly engage the notches. There shouldn't be any movement at all. With the drawer in place, check the other end to make sure the edges of 5, 6 and 7 are properly flush with that of the outside case. If they are, pop some glue on their edges and attach piece 11 to them. When it's dry, you can pin this too. You should now have the completed inner secret drawer and most of the outer case.

To finish up, you need to cut the beading. You may as well do it all at once as well. You'll need eight pieces 6 in. (152 mm) long and 16 bits that are 3 in. (76 mm) long. When you cut the beading it's important that every angle is at exactly 45 degrees so that the corners fit together perfectly and hide the box's secrets. Fix and pin the beading to the top and sides of the outer case. Then remove the drawer and attach the beading to the front of piece 11. When that's dry, replace the drawer and glue and pin

the final four pieces of beading to the outside back of the box. It is very important that these final pieces are not attached to the inner panel (10). When the box is finished, you should be able to slide down the panel (10) to release the catches and then open the secret drawer.

Fig. 165. *The two hooks on the end of the drawer will slip over the catches shown in Fig. 164.*

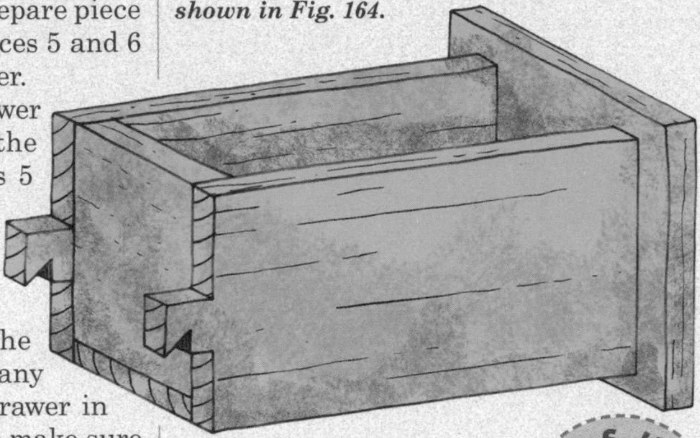

The Private Shed

In the past, many sheds have been used as the "smallest room in the house," to use the quaint euphemism for a bathroom. And the bathroom, it seems, is making a comeback, particularly in the U.S. Visitors to one truly bizarre website will find the home of the Official Outhouses Of America Tour, which is packed with photographs of out-houses—single and double holers—past and present from all over North America. The most bizarre is probably the indoor outhouse—an outside toilet built inside somebody's house!

GLOSSARY

Armature Two meanings for this. First, it's a piece of soft iron connecting the poles of a magnet; second, it's a framework for a clay sculpture.

Awl A sharp, hand-held pointed tool, used for making holes in wood to "start off" a nail or screw.

Batten A narrow strip of wood.

Beading A strip of wood with one flat edge and one moulded edge, used for decoration and to conceal "gappy" woodwork.

Bevel To cut a slope in wood or metal at an angle of anything other than 90 degrees; chisels have a bevelled edge.

Brad A finishing nail with a small head, usually only up to 25 mm (1 in) long.

Bradawl A small awl, designed for use with brads.

Burr A rough edge, left on a piece of metal like a chisel blade, after it's been sharpened.

Butt joint Literally, the joint you get when you "butt" two pieces of wood squarely against each other.

Calico Plain white cotton cloth useful for making kites, sails and so on.

Chamfer Used by many interchangeably with "bevel," it means to cut off the edge or corner of a piece of wood or metal at an angle other than 90 degrees.

Coach bolt A bolt with a square "collar" under the head which is designed to bite into wood and then lock into position when you tighten it. You'll usually find a washer being used to stop the nut at the other end sinking into the wood.

Concave A shape that curves inwards (remember it by thinking of the "cave" in concave).

Convex A shape that bends outwards (easy to remember because it's the opposite of "concave").

Cotter pin A special fastening pin with a split shaft. You push it through a hole and then splay the shaft open to secure the pin.

Countersink A tool designed to enlarge the top part of a hole such that the head of a screw lies flush with the surface of the wood.

Dado A rectangular channel or groove cut into a piece of wood designed to take a second piece of wood of the same thickness as the channel.

Dovetail joint A way of joining wood at corners, by the use of interlocking pins and tails, that's very secure and good to look at.

Dowel A small, preformed wooden pin that's glued into a hole and used to reinforce a wood joint.

Field coil An electrical coil around a magnet that's used in an electric motor to generate a magnetic field.

Formalin A mixture of formaldehyde and water, used here to harden a photograph, which you can buy from a pharmacist. Always follow the instructions and handle with care.

Fretsaw A narrow-bladed saw used for making fine cuts in thin wood—see Fretwork.

Fretwork Ornamental wood carving that creates a decorative lattice inside a thin piece of wood. This is then glued onto the surface of a larger piece.

G-clamp A mechanical clamp designed to hold pieces of wood together while glue sets. So called because it has a "G" shape.

Gelatin A curious transparent animal protein that's used in food and photographic development.

Gnomon The part of a sundial that casts a shadow and is used as an indicator.

Gouge Looks like a chisel but has a rounded blade, a bit like a trough. Used for digging out wood either in carving or to create a hollow section.

Grain The size, alignment, and color of wood fibers in a piece of wood.

Hardboard Softwood pulp that's forced into sheets under high pressure. Has one smooth side.

Hardwood Wood from broad-leaved trees that's harder to cut and longer-lasting than softwood.

Head bolt A bit like an overweight screw, this has a six-sided hole in the top that is designed to be quick and easy to tighten.

Honing The action of removing fine scratches and burrs from the head of a tool that may remain after sharpening.

Inlay Thin wood, arranged in an attractive design and then set into thicker wood so that it lays flush with the surface.

Locked nut Two nuts on a bolt that are tightened against each other.

Miter Refers to a corner joint where two pieces of wood are bevelled at 45 degrees to form a single 90-degree corner.

Miter block A block of wood with grooves in it designed to help you cut accurate angles for miter joints.

Mortise A rectangular hole in a piece of wood designed to receive a tenon (a same-sized "tongue" of wood) to form a joint.

Oilstone A whetstone, lubricated with oil, used for sharpening and honing.

Panel pin A small nail used for fixing thin pieces of wood together.

Plane A handheld tool with an adjustable blade, used for smoothing and levelling wood.

Plywood Made by bonding layers of veneer together in various thicknesses.

Rebate A groove cut along the edge of a piece of wood designed to take a second piece of wood to make a joint.

Sheet-metal shop A metalworking firm that will make one-off parts. Your local hardware store will be able to recommend one.

Shooting board Device used to ensure that wood is planed perfectly square.

Softwood Commonly used for indoor projects (if used outdoors it will need protecting)—for example, pine.

Solder An alloy usually made of lead and tin that can be heated and used to fuse metals together.

Starch paste Used as a primitive adhesive and thickener—made from one part white starch and three parts water.

Stack-dried wood The proper way to store hardwood outside.

SWG Standard Wire Gauge is the accepted way to measure the width of wire.

Tenon A "tongue" of wood sticking out from a board that fits into a matching mortise to make a joint.

INDEX

Project 47
Spring-trap Car,
page 60

Project 96 Bird
Box, page 117

*Technique 3 Nailing,
    Screwing and Gluing,
    page 10*

*Project 29 Nature's
Bookmarks, page 40*

*Project 56
Scarecrow,
page 69*

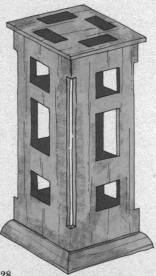

*Project 26 Toothbrush
Stand, page 37*